D1214216

LET LIFE BEGIN

A LIRISS Book / Published by arrangement with the author

For information address: LIRISS Books Publishing,
3432 Wythe House Cove
Bartlett, TN 38134
Or E-mail:
Rick45@aol.com

ISBN: 0-9722315-0-1

A LIRISS BOOK
LIRISS Books are published by Richard L. Jacobs, Sr.
3432 Wythe House Cove
Bartlett, TN 38134

PRINTED IN THE UNITED STATES OF AMERICA

10 9 8 7 6 5 4 3 2 1

DEDICATION

I dedicate this to my wife and my children. I would never have made it through without them. To Susie, thank-you for living and knowing who I am. To my three boys, Ricky, Jr., Sean and Scotty, thank-you for your love and unconditional support at a time where I would have expected and understood much less. And especially to my daughter, Lisa, who has stepped up and taken over so many duties that Susie used to do. I have come to depend on her and she has surpassed my wildest expectations.

I also wish to thank my immediate family, particularly my two sisters, Becky and Terri, and my sister-in-law, Sandy. The hot meals continue to arrive from these wonderful people, and they have maintained almost daily contact with Susie, even many months later. Without their help, life would be so much harder. I further wish to express my sincere appreciation to Mike and Gretchen for their support and loyalty during a time when it was so sorely needed. And to my sister-in-law, and Susie's sister, Jan, who has always been one of my favorite people. I realize the strain you have been under. I value your support more than you can possibly imagine. Finally, to my dear friend Beth, I love you. That's all I can say.

To all the doctors and nurses at Methodist North Hospital and at HealthSouth Rehabilitation Hospital, especially Scott, Rhonda, Vonda, Debbie, Keith, Sharon, Brenda, Timeka, Susan, Carolyn and a host of others that I know I'm forgetting, thank-you for your dedication and skill. Susie is alive today because of you. To Dr. David Wright, a close friend and fellow musician, thank-you for all of your help and free medical advice. It is so nice to have friends in high places.

To the teachers and administrators at Bartlett Elementary, Elmore Park Middle School and Bartlett High, thank-you for your help and understanding. My kids were able to miss many

1

days to be with their mom, and it helped them tremendously. Special thanks go to Ms. Crawford, Scotty's kindergarten teacher. She took him under her wing; a wing that without question belongs to an angel.

I would be remiss not to include my editor, Grace, in this dedication. This is my first book, and her encouragement and expertise was indeed valuable. You are truly amazing, Grace.

To all of those who put Susie on their prayer lists, thank-you. Prayer is the reason she is with us today, and continued prayer will help her improve and give me the strength necessary to rise and face each and every day.

And finally, thank-you God. Your existence is, for the first time in my life, unmistakable.

FOREWORD

"It was the best of times, it was the worst of times." (C. Dickens)

"Life is difficult." (M.S. Peck)

"In the beginning..."

All of these are opening lines of great books, any of which would be appropriate for THIS great book. You are about to be led on a journey of discovery by one of the most passionately honest and caring men I have ever had the pleasure of knowing personally. You will be taken into this family's inner sanctum as they experience a crisis of epic proportions. You will learn why the Chinese character representing "crisis" aptly combines their characters for "danger" and "opportunity" into one. You will be privileged to see what true love in action entails. And finally, you will witness one man's discovery of God in the midst of crisis. The story continues far beyond these pages.

This powerful book will have a universal appeal. As an internist with more than twenty years experience in these matters, I highly recommend it to: Laymen, who are very likely to face a similar predicament, since half of all deaths are from cardiovascular diseases; to health care professionals - doctors, nurses, laboratory technicians, radiology technicians, ward clerks and housekeepers - who care for these patients and all too often forget the human ramifications of their decisions on the suffering patient and family; to medical institutions of learning, who need to pass these truths on to the next generation of professionals BEFORE they are confronted by the situation.

Prepare to be deeply moved and profoundly affected.

Let life begin.

David B. Wright, M.D.

PROLOGUE

When I look back over the last few months of my life, it doesn't seem real.

The reason it doesn't seem real is because the events, which have occurred since the morning of September 5, 2001, only happen in dreams. Or to other people. You read about, or hear about, so and so's wife having a massive heart attack. And, wow! What a shame! They have four kids, and a business, and a wonderful marriage and she's only 39! How could that happen at such a young age? And you shake your head and mumble your condolences to no one in particular and then go about your life otherwise unshaken.

My family and I, however, didn't have that luxury. My wife's heart attack was real. The words in the previous paragraph undoubtedly were whispered in horror and shock. But they were whispered by other people who heard about my wife and, as I, simply could not believe it.

Our world - and whenever I say "our" I mean my entire family: Susie, our four children, and myself - forever changed on that Wednesday morning. Priorities, relationships, plans, emotions, spirituality - nearly every aspect of life as we knew it. It was the unthinkable, the unimaginable and the nightmare that you will wake up from at any moment all rolled into one. The morning of September 5th was the beginning of a roller coaster of emotions that took me from the absolute depth of despair to heights of euphoria and everything in between. I learned what unconditional love was all about. I learned as well how a boiling pot of agony and anger could nearly erase close relationships, and eventually erupt into an atmosphere of hostility and explosiveness. I learned what miracles God is capable of. And I especially learned a lot about my children and me.

There are still issues I cannot resolve and which I may never fully understand. This is the reason I decided to write this story. Maybe there were further silver linings to this that I would be able to add to those already found. Maybe, just maybe, by reawakening some of the moments when I felt so utterly betrayed by life and by God, I'd be able to understand some of those issues. And finally, through writing, I would be able to fully explain thoughts and emotions which led me to heartbreaking decisions that no one should have to make about a loved one. Decisions which, thank God Almighty, never had to be carried out.

I hope as well that Susie will not have suffered completely in vain. If I am fortunate enough to see this work published, I pray that readers will appreciate the incredible gift of time, and will use this gift wisely. Appreciate your spouse and loved ones, and understand that time is not a guarantee. Say "I love you" more often. Spend quality time together. Hold hands, kiss regularly, and enjoy your families. Also, review your life and health insurance now and make sure they are adequate before it is too late. And, by all means, consider disability insurance, regardless of your age. Don't let hindsight find you wishing you had. I wish I had listened to my agent a little more closely.

I don't know exactly what the future holds for my family and me. The only way I'll ever know is to wait for it. My faith in God will sustain me until then. In the meantime, I will continue to write. Writing is enormously therapeutic. It restores sanity in an otherwise insane world. It helps put in perspective my new role in life: take care of a loved one who is no longer able to take care of herself, and then have enough faith in God, and in Susie, to do everything in my power to help her get better.

Is the written word really this powerful?

Oh, my, yes! Without question, it is indeed!

CHAPTER ONE:

THE FIRST TWENTY YEARS

The first time I met Susie was at my parent's drycleaners. She was young, cute, and curvy, with a smile that to this day makes me melt.

The way I first heard about Susie was as unique as our relationship. The last letter that I received from my mother as a U.S. serviceman in England mentioned the new neighbors who had moved in next door. She then proceeded to write that they had a daughter who I would likely want to get to know. I remember distinctly, after reading this, being anxious to get home to meet this girl. Perhaps it had something to do with the fact that my mother didn't like very many of my girlfriends, and here she was more or less playing matchmaker. I was intrigued, and for the entire month I had left overseas my mind remained occupied on a girl I had yet to meet.

As I have discovered more and more as the years go by, my mother was one smart lady. The first time I met Susie was at my parent's dry-cleaners. It was February 10, 1979, the day after I returned home from overseas. She was young, cute, and curvy, with a smile that to this day makes me melt. She also had a boyfriend. However, this would prove to be less of a problem than I had thought at the time. Apparently she liked what she saw as well. I'll never understand it - I guess love truly is blind.

Her parents didn't approve of Susie's choice at first. It was understandable. I was too old - five and one half years older than Susie to be exact - and I wasn't Catholic. This would be a problem from time to time during the nearly two years we dated. My in-laws good points far outweighed the bad, however, and I have considered myself lucky to have them as family.

We were married on November 14, 1980. We honeymooned in Florida and then settled down to a marriage made in heaven. As in all marriages, we had our share of problems and bad times, particularly at the beginning. I was far from perfect, and living together, we would learn, was not the same as dating. But we worked through these problems. We discovered that getting along was far more fun than fighting and arguing. I can honestly state that not once in our 21 years of marriage has divorce ever been discussed or given a serious thought. Ours was a special relationship, one that comes along so rarely, especially in a time when separation and divorce is the norm rather than the exception. I made it my responsibility to understand that Susie's decision to spend her one and only life with me was very special. She would never regret that decision.

Our most glorious moments were the births of our four children. Lisa on January 17, 1983; Ricky, Jr. on November 12, 1985; Sean on March 21, 1990; and finally little Scotty, our surprise baby, on August 29, 1995. We love to tell the story about Scotty and how he was nearly named "You're WHAT?" All four kids are different; all four are special in their own way. We are very proud of each of them.

Our fifth glorious moment occurred on January 29, 2000. After months of planning and watching an agonizingly slow building process, we opened our own business. We called it "Simply The Best Cleaners" and, in a way, it was like watching another baby being born. We worked 80 hours a week, nurturing and nursing our dream. Our kids were always with us, especially during the summer months. We sweated the slow times and celebrated each and every new milestone realized. In the eighteenth month, our business was finally beginning to do well, really well. We were at last able to see the light at the end of a very long and arduous tunnel. The long hours and incredibly hard work was paying off, and the American dream was going to be reality.

Our life was good. We loved each other and our family. We were a team. We could work all day together and still be happy to see one another the next morning. We seldom let a day go by without saying "I love you". I've told my kids that if they found a mate they could love half as much as I love their mother, they would be very fortunate. We loved being together and doing things. We could fish for hours and hours on our pier on the lakefront property we owned and never tire of it. We took family vacations, and we had several wonderful trips together without the kids. With us, the honeymoon was never over. We were made for only each other. The thought of growing old with any other person was never a possibility. We had such plans for the future.

I have to write that again. We had such plans for the future.

But then, on September 5, 2001, everything changed.

CHAPTER TWO:

SEPTEMBER 5TH

"Clear!"

Her body shuddered. The silence was deafening. My own heart nearly stopped.

"Still no pulse!"

I wonder if there lives a writer who is so gifted, so magical with words, so incredibly talented with his craft that he would be able to express the complete and utter anguish and helplessness that I felt on September 5th. I've tried to explain it to others. I've relived the horror literally hundreds of times over the last few months. It remains as fresh as if it just happened an instant ago. To attempt to describe the emotions that you go through as you witness your wife literally die in your arms would be useless. It cannot be done. There are no words in the world, in any language or dialect, that could describe what cannot be described.

One would think that the person who has the heart attack is the one who suffers. I disagree. Susie remembers nothing before or during the attack and very little after. The vast majority of the suffering is done by family members as they try to endure the agonizingly slow hours and days following the attack as the healing process hopefully runs its course. I do not try to minimize my wife's horrible experience, yet it is a fact that she remained mercifully sedated and asleep through most of the really difficult times. Those who love her, however, had to deal with the situation with open eyes.

Looking back, I now realize the first inkling of what was to come happened shortly after midnight on that Wednesday morning. I awoke to find my wife sitting straight up in bed, her hand on her chest and her breathing labored. She was obviously in pain.

"What's wrong, sweetie?" I asked the question more out of obligation than concern. She had had these pains for nearly a year and doctors had told us that it was nothing more than acid reflux.

Between breaths, and in a voice that got my attention, she said, "My chest really hurts, Rick, and I'm having trouble catching my breath."

I sat up and put my arm around her. "Should we go to the

hospital? When's the last time you took one of your pills?" She had been prescribed Prevacid for the reflux which she had failed to take to completion.

"No, not yet. Let me see what happens." She sounded a little better. "This has happened before. It'll go away in a minute."

I'm reasonably certain I fell back asleep before her pains stopped because the next thing I knew my alarm went off. I looked over at her and she was sleeping peacefully, her breathing easy and steady. I was satisfied that she was fine and proceeded to get ready for work. We had a routine, Susie and me, where I would leave the house two or three hours earlier than she to open up the cleaners, get loads of laundry started, and generally prepare for the day. She would sleep a little longer and get the boys up and dressed, fed and off to the bus stop hopefully before the bus got there. We were happy working together this way. I didn't mind getting up early - she loved to sleep. I was raised to understand that the man of the house did the bulk of the work away from the home, and she was brought up in a loving home where her mom was always there. It was important to us that, while we worked sometimes superhuman hours at our business, the kids still had at least one parent at home, at least part time, to check homework, work on projects, sign papers - whatever.

I called her later that morning, although it wasn't only to see how she was feeling. I always called her before she left for work just to check on how her morning was going. Normally I would get a report on which son she was ready to strangle. I asked her if she was still in pain.

"No, I really feel fine. I tell you, though, last night I really thought I was having a heart attack." She sounded perfectly normal.

As I wrote earlier, she had chest pains less than a year earlier. Severe chest pains. We took her immediately to the hospital. We were told that it was acid reflux, pure and simple. No heart problems whatsoever. We were never led to believe it could be anything except acid reflux. How I wish this had been the first pains she experienced; The rest of this story would not need to be told.

I hung up and never gave it another thought. She drove up at her usual time and began tagging clothes. We were extremely busy, both in the front and back in the production area. It was the Wednesday after the long Labor Day weekend, and we were covered up in clothes. I was in the back loading machines and hanging up clothes to be pressed. About 9:30 I went up front to check on the tagging progress. Susie was sitting down in our private office, her forehead resting on one hand, her other hand on her chest.

"What's wrong, Susie?" I knew her answer before she told me, of course. Her chest hurt. This was no secret. I was more irritated than concerned. I come from a family that, even if we were sick, we worked. There was seldom sympathy. God knows, with the benefit of hindsight, I wish I had acted differently towards her. But, we were busy, really busy! And I needed her marking in, not sitting in the office. "Did you take one of your pills this morning?"

"No, I forgot." She began to cry. That always worked with me.

"You forgot? Baby, how could you forget, especially after last night?"

"I just forgot. Can I go get one?"

I'm not sure if I went home and got her pill or if I called our daughter and she brought one. Our business was less than two miles from our home. Bottom line is, she was able to get one of her Prevacids quickly and it seemed to help. She went back to work feeling much better.

Susie was back in our office, however, less than one hour later, and in much worse pain. It seemed nearly as severe as the first time she experienced her chest pains months earlier. Her mom had an appointment to get her hair done at a salon next door to the cleaners, and had stopped by to chat beforehand. She sat with Susie while I paged a doctor friend of mine. She was concerned, but knew as well as I that these were the same pains that were diagnosed as reflux. She kept her appointment, promising to return as soon as she was done.

As soon as her mom left, I asked, "Susie, is there a chance you can get back to work any time soon?" She responded with words that will haunt me for the rest of my life. "Rick, my chest hurts so bad. I'm really afraid I'm having a heart attack, and I don't want to die."

I was stunned. She was crying again. I went back to the phone. My doctor friend hadn't returned my page - I later found out he was out of town - and I called Susie's brother, Jimmy. He was a paramedic and I wanted his opinion. I got him on his cell phone.

"Jimmy, it's Rick. I got a medical question for you. Can acid reflux hurt so badly that Susie is in tears and can't work?"

"Rick," as always, he carefully selected his words, "sometimes it can. I tell you what, bring her into the station tomorrow morning and we'll hook her up again. I'll be back on duty and it won't be a problem."

"OK, Jimmy. We'll see you then." He would later struggle mightily with his advice to us, but there was no way we blamed him for what happened later to his sister. Like us, he was trusting what physicians had told us months earlier. I hope one day he'll come to terms with what happened and be at peace. I've seen his pain, and I fear he is bearing the heavy burden of guilt. It's not his fault. It is no one's fault.

I left Susie in the office and went to finish the marking in, resigned that Susie was unable to work at least for the time being. The pains had become bearable again but not to the point of returning to work. It took probably another 45 minutes or so to finish tagging the morning's work. I stuck my head in the office door to see how she was feeling. Her mother was back from the beauty shop and sitting with her again. "The sooner you can come to the back the better!" I said, then I went to the back myself.

She did come back briefly and folded a few sweaters, but I could tell she wasn't 100%. She was moving very slowly, and it was obvious that she was in pain. God love her, she was trying. I knew it was only a matter of time before she was going to tell me she was going home. With her mom there, I knew I would have to let her. She left the back area and was in our office again.

It was only minutes before her mom came to find me. She looked worried. "Rick, something's really wrong with Susie. I'm taking her to the hospital."

The look in her eyes and the way she spoke let me know that there was no argument here. "OK, I'm going with you."

She said, "No, you're busy. You get caught up, and I'll call you when we find out what the doctor says."

I let her go. One of my pressers asked me what was going on. I told her that Susie's mom was taking her to the hospital. "It's going to be nothing but a bad case of acid reflux again, and it'll cost me $500 for something I already know," I said. She nodded her head understandingly. God knows I have struggled with making that statement. I should have insisted on going with them or taking her myself. I should have taken her the night before. We should have known that acid reflux would not cause the pain she was enduring. I should have been more sympathetic. I should have taken better care of her.

Isn't that my job? To take care of my family? I promised her that from the beginning - that I would always take care of her. I let her down, and there was not a damn thing I can do about it.

I thought Susie's mom had left to take her to the hospital.

It was maybe a couple of minutes later when one of my employees came to the back and informed me that I was needed up front. I thought a customer had a question he couldn't answer. When I arrived up front, there was a customer on the other side of the counter, and I cheerfully asked what I could do for her.

She pointed towards my office. "I think they need you in there."

Through the open office door, I saw my wife falling to the floor, her mom attempting to hold her up, one hand grabbing a handful of blouse just below her neck, her other hand clinging to the phone, fighting hysterics and panic. I rushed in and grabbed Susie, and was shocked to notice how stiff she was. Her eyes were rolled back into her head, and there was only a breath or two while I carefully laid her to the floor. They weren't ordinary breaths, but loud and forced through closed lips. Then there were no breaths at all.

I can not tell you how long it took before I realized exactly what was happening to her. I only know that when I first understood that she was having a heart attack it was as if I really was in a dream - or nightmare. I became aware that her mom was talking to 911, and she asked, "Rick, is Susie breathing?"

In my mind I wanted to scream, "Of course she's breathing! Why are you asking me this? This is my 39-year-old wife, not my 89-year-old grandmother!" Somehow, I fought pure, unbridled panic and listened for any sounds of breathing. There were none. "No, she's not!" I cried, "Susie, for God's sakes, breathe!"

"Rick," her mother pleaded, "you've got to breathe for her!" And so I gave my wife mouth-to-mouth. At first, when she would automatically expel the breaths I gave to her, I thought she had begun breathing on her own again. "There you go, baby! You're breathing! She's breathing, Mom!" I cried! Then, again, there would be nothing but silence, until it finally dawned on me what was happening. So, I kept breathing for her. She'd be OK, I reasoned, as long as I breathed for her.

Then Susie's mom asked a question that goes beyond the scope of reasonable questions. She asked me if there was a pulse. The reality of that question hit me like a semi head on. In other words, was Susie still alive? How could she ask a question like that? How could anyone reasonably expect me to answer? What did she mean, was there a pulse? She was asking me if her heart was still beating. *Her heart!* I checked her wrist. I couldn't tell if there was a pulse or not. I didn't want to stop the mouth to mouth. "Mom," I said, "I don't know!" The customer who had been up front heard everything that was going on. She came into the office and knelt down beside Susie.

"I've had some training, Rick. I'll check for a pulse. You keep breathing for her." She put her fingers on Susie's wrist, and we all waited. She looked at Susie's mom and shook her head.

All I heard next were prayers. "Dear Lord, help this sweet child. Put your healing hand on her and bring her back." I didn't want to hear this. I kept breathing for her.

"Mom!" I said between breaths, "how long before the paramedics get here?"

"They're on their way, Rick!"

"She's not breathing, Mom! She has no pulse!"

"I know, Rick!" - she was crying now - "They'll be here any minute!"

"Tell 'em to hurry, God, please tell 'em to hurry!! Susie, don't leave us. Please don't leave us. Breathe, please God, breathe. Oh, God, this is not happening!!"

But it was happening. While we kept up the CPR as well as humanly possible under the circumstances - try giving effective CPR to your spouse - it was becoming more and more clear to me that Susie might die. She might already be dead. I found that, even though there is a place in your brain that is rational enough to understand this, it was impossible for me to accept it. It seemed an eternity, but the sirens from the ambulance could be heard. It was then with great relief that I let the trained experts take over. She'll get better now. They will make her better. This is what they do.

Immediately the paramedics gave her oxygen and checked her pulse. I watched a scene that was right out of the 911 television series. Yet, this was not TV. This was really happening, and it was happening to me. I heard one of the paramedics say, "I've got no pulse." I nearly fainted. In seconds they were ready to shock Susie.

"CLEAR!"

Her body shuddered. The silence was deafening. My own heart nearly stopped.

"Still no pulse!"

Crushed, I began to wail, "Oh, God, no, Susie, please!!!" The paramedics asked that someone take me out of the room. One of my employees tried to pull me back. I shook her arm away. "I'm not leaving her. Let go!" She let go. I looked at one of the paramedics with eyes that both pleaded and promised that I would regain my composure. They went back to work.

"CLEAR!"

No pulse. A third time no pulse. And a fourth. Finally, when I had all but given up, I heard one of them say, "All right! I've got a pulse!!"

The real paramedic work started then. IVs went in, shots given - four or five people were working on her all at the same time and all of them working as one. I felt relieved enough to start thinking at least somewhat clearly. I called my brother-in-law, Lee, to come and watch the store for me. I called

Susie's brother, Jimmy, and my two sisters. I asked my employees to try and finish the day while I went to the hospital with Susie. Then I called my daughter at nursing school. She cried and said she'd see me at the hospital. It was then I cried, and I told her I'd see her there.

I rode in the front seat of the ambulance. My Susie rode in the back, barely clinging to life. Four or five strangers worked to keep her alive, along with her brother, while we drove to the hospital. Her heart stopped again on the way and was still in total defibrillation when we arrived at the emergency room. No one expected her to make it. Thank God I didn't know it at the time.

We pulled into the hospital. I got out and watched in horror as they got her out of the ambulance and wheeled her into the ER. I leaned against a column and slumped down to the ground. The ache in my stomach was unbearable. I was afraid to go in. The tears began to flow. I didn't know it then, but this was the beginning of the longest six weeks of my life. My world as I knew it was gone. My wife would never be the same. More would happen to me in the next 43 days than I could have ever imagined.

Jesus once asked, "My God, why have you forsaken me?" He felt alone, empty, helpless and was experiencing unimaginable pain.

I wonder what God said to comfort him.

CHAPTER THREE:

THE EMERGENCY ROOM

It was wonderful that someone thought to call the church, but then the cold realization of what he was doing hit me. He was praying for her, true enough, but the prayers were her Last Rites.

It was nearly more than I could handle.

I got up and walked through the automatic doors and into the emergency room. Susie was not in sight. There was a nurse behind a counter who looked up when I entered. I walked up to her and asked if I could see Susie.

"Patient's full name?" Indifference. Just another day at the office.

"Susan Jacobs." She began looking through paperwork on the desk in front of her. I told her that she had just been brought in by ambulance. "She had a heart attack. Can I please go see her?"

She stopped looking. "What is your relation to the patient?"

Through tear filled eyes, and in a voice barely above a whisper, I said, "She's my wife."

Her demeanor immediately softened. She became compassionate and motherly. "OK honey, I'll go check on her. While I'm gone, I need to ask you to go the booth over there and answer some questions for us, OK?" I nodded and walked over to where she had pointed. A different nurse was seated behind a desk with some forms ready. I anticipated endless questions about insurance, names and addresses, place of employment, and on and on. It took less than 30 seconds, however, and I was grateful. Apparently they knew I was unable to think of little else besides Susie. They would get the information later.

The nurse behind the counter was back. I looked at her hopefully. "They're still with her, Mr. Jacobs. Please have a seat over in the waiting room. They'll come and get you as soon as they can." I looked over to where she was pointing, and nodded. She then added, "She's in excellent hands, Mr. Jacobs." Again I nodded, then walked away.

Some of our families had already begun to arrive, tears and hugs were everywhere. Condolences and encouragements were being whispered as well as words of shock and disbelief.

I sat down, not wanting to talk to anyone, and stared at the door where I knew a doctor would come through and give us news of Susie. We have all seen doctors talking to families countless times on TV and in movies. We've seen them deliver bad news. Sometimes you won't even hear the dialogue - just mournful music. The spouse or parents then collapse to the floor, sobbing uncontrollably. We all know what the doctor said - the patient didn't make it. And then we feel sad for the survivors. Isn't that funny? We feel sorry for actors who get paid to do the scene. No one actually died, yet we are emotional. You can imagine the emotion in this waiting room where a real life spouse waited and a loved one was barely clinging to life somewhere in the ER.

I tried to imagine what was happening to Susie. I pictured wires and lines being hooked up to her. I could hear doctors shouting orders one after the other, and nurses, somehow knowing which orders were theirs, following them.

I then pictured her doctor coming through the door with a grim look, and giving me bad news. Over and over again this scenario played in my head. I don't know why. He would tell me that she didn't make it, and then I would collapse to the floor, the kindly doctor's hand on my shoulder in comfort. Was I subconsciously preparing myself for the worst? Possibly. Yet, I actually dreaded the arrival of whoever would come in with news of Susie. You see, as long as I didn't know anything, she was still alive. Once they told me, whatever they told me, it was final.

The door finally did open, and a doctor came through. I stood up and looked at him expectantly. He was young, full of energy and did not appear to have the look of a bearer of really bad news.

He looked at me. "Mr. Jacobs?" I nodded. "Your wife is alive. Would you like to see her?"

I almost fell to the floor, the relief was so overwhelming.

Family members behind me, hearing the same thing I heard, began sobbing in relief and giving thanks to God. I followed the doctor back to see Susie. I was the only one allowed to see her at this time. He began to prepare me.

"She's had a rough time, and she's going to look it. Be ready. She has lots of machines hooked up to her. Right now we have to breathe for her. You can only see her for a minute before we take her upstairs for x-rays."

"Is she going to be OK?"

"It's too soon to tell. We'll know more after the x-rays and a dye injection."

We entered a room and, through a window, I saw Susie for the first time inside the hospital. It was terrible. She lay on a bed, a breathing tube down her throat and into her lungs. Countless wires and tubes were all over her body. Her eyes were closed, and she was not moving. Nurses and doctors were prodding her, giving her shots and setting equipment up all around to keep her alive. Her face was barely recognizable, and I had to fight to keep my composure. There was a chair in the room, and I sat down on it. Then the doctor's hand was on my shoulder. "We'll be taking her upstairs in just a minute. We'll know a lot more at that point."

"Can I go up with her?" I could barely talk.

He considered that for a moment. "OK."

We left and went into the room where Susie lay clinging to life. I walked over to her bed and found her hand. I held it ever so gently for fear of hurting her, and called her name. "Susie. It's me, sweetie. Can you hear me?" I knew she couldn't answer, but I was so hoping she could hear me. I hoped it would help her to hear my voice.

We began moving, with everyone working together to move machinery and IVs along with Susie. I never let go of her hand; I never stopped talking to her. I then noticed that a priest from our church, Father Joseph, was walking with us and saying prayers. I was glad to see him. It was wonderful that someone thought to call the church, but then the cold realization of what he was doing hit me. He was praying for her, true enough, but the prayers were her Last Rites. It was nearly more than I could handle.

We entered an elevator and went up. The only sound was Father Joe quietly praying. Susie lay perfectly still, her eyes still closed and her warm hand still in mine. The elevator stopped, and we moved again as soon as the doors opened. We came to double doors, and I was told it was as far as I could go. They allowed Father Joe to continue on with them. I watched through windows in the door until they turned a corner and were out of sight. My wife was in the hands of total strangers. I had no control whatsoever of her immediate care. I could make no decisions, offer no advice. All I could do was pray that those who were now with her would take care of her the way I would had I the training. I somehow managed to find my way back to the waiting room, and did my best answering the many questions from family members.

At some point during the course of the rest of the day I was shown a picture of her heart. The cardiologist on duty brought it up on a computer. The artery down the front and middle of her heart, before the stents were installed, was maybe a half-inch long. This was the before picture. She then showed me the after picture. The cardiologist had installed two stents, which would remain in Susie's artery for the rest of her life. The artery was several inches long now and had branches of veins all along the way to the bottom of her heart. It was as if a dam had been built and then torn down. It had very nearly cost Susie her life, and it still could very easily. It would be touch and go for at least 48 hours, the cardiologist told me. If she survived 48 hours, the chances increased dramatically that she would live.

She would be taken to the Cardiovascular Intensive Care Unit next. She would remain there for the next eight days.

CHAPTER FOUR:

THE CARDIOVASCULAR INTENSIVE CARE UNIT

The reality of the situation was I had no earthly idea what the future held. It was this horrible fear of the unknown that would haunt me every hour of every day we were there.

It haunts me even today.

The Cardiovascular Intensive Care Unit. It's where you go if you are in imminent danger of dying from some sort of heart disease.

This is where Susie was taken just a few hours after two stents were placed in her heart. There is only one way to describe the CVICU: Scary. Very scary.

There are machines everywhere: heart monitors, machines that breathe for you, feed you, administer medicine, and machines that keep close tabs on your temperature, blood pressure and oxygen level. After a while you get used to them, but at first, when you have no idea what they all are, you feel overwhelmed.

Getting accustomed to the alarms are the hardest part. At first, every time a bell or whistle goes off, you freak. Oh my God, something's wrong!! And you wonder why three or four people aren't storming in to Harvey Team your loved one back to life. Usually a nurse will eventually walk in and casually press a button on one of the machines and then walk back out without a word. Toward the end of Susie's stay in the CVICU I had been shown which alarms were harmless, and I was allowed to reset them myself. I got to where I hated all the alarms. I would dream about them during the few minutes at a time I was able to sleep.

Once Susie was in her room I was allowed back. It was awful. A breathing tube remained down her throat and into her lungs. That, far and away, was the worst part for her and for us. A machine breathed for her. You could hear it click and whirr and watch her chest rise up and down with it. There was a bite guard around the tube and it forced her mouth wide open. Eventually her lips would get cracked and dry from it, and sores formed where her lips came in contact with it. I kept ChapStick and Vaseline on her. It was one of the very few things I could do for her, and it helped take an edge off the incredible feeling of helplessness I felt, and would feel for weeks. The breathing tube was a never-ending nightmare for Susie. Once she became aware of it, it scared the hell out of her. Her gag reflex tried to throw it up. Her eyes pleaded with whoever was in the room to take it out. When she would cough, there was no sound except for a muffled air noise from inside the tube. The removal of the tube became our first priority for her. We knew, if only psychologically, that this could do as much good for her as any medicine or treatment.

Wires and IV tubes were everywhere. Computer monitors displayed her heartbeat. It was profoundly sobering to know that the peaks and valleys on the screen were Susie's, and that they were being carefully and continually watched. She had IV ports in the veins on the top of both hands and in her neck. Drugs were being administered from several soft plastic bags situated above her and through machines that were set for the proper dosage. Eventually, I was able to read and understand the numbers and settings on most of the equipment in Susie's room, and this was a tremendous help to me. I never was able to get over the fact that Susie's very life depended on this equipment working properly. There is equipment in my business. They break down occasionally. The complexity of the electronics in this room was mind-boggling. It was keeping the most important person in my and my kid's world alive. Obviously, everything worked as promised. I wish I could fill out a customer satisfaction card. Thank you, Siemans.

There was a male nurse in the room when I came in the very first time. His name was Scott. He was young, probably not yet 30, and he would prove to be one of the most compassionate human beings I have ever had the pleasure of knowing. It takes a special person to be a nurse. It takes someone superhuman to be an ICU nurse. All of the nurses who would care for Susie were so extraordinary that I wonder how the hospital was able to assemble them in one unit. It's almost as if they ran a want ad that read, "Help wanted - ICU Nurses. Only the phenomenally gifted and capable need apply. Must never have bad moments. The patience of Job a must. Must be able to listen to patient's husband ramble for hours without interruption."

This, in a small way, describes the staff of the unit Susie was in. I don't know what I would have done without them. They went beyond superior care. Susie was not just another patient. She was a person, flesh and blood, with family and friends, and they never forgot it. They understood that I was a distraught husband who desperately needed to ask questions, visit past the strict hours and just talk about Susie and our life together. Without exception, they were all of this. Their care of Susie extended to me. I will forever be grateful.

We decorated Susie's room with several picture collages. Each collage had pictures from different parts of her life. Holidays, parties, vacations and special occasions from both sides of the family were on display. We did this for Susie. We hoped that she would wake up soon and want to see them. What we didn't know was how much the nurses would enjoy them. They made it a point to tell us how important it was for them to be reminded that Susie was loved and that she had family and friends who wanted her home again. She had a life to get back to. I spent hours with all of the nurses going over each and every picture. It was wonderful therapy for me.

The first night in the waiting room is a fog. There were so many visitors between family and friends that we filled most of the room. I was in a daze. I kept waiting and wanting to wake up. Someone would walk up to me, give me a hug and offer their condolences, encouragement and help, then go around the room to other family members and friends to repeat the ritual.

I remembered at some point that first afternoon that I had not called my parents. They were retired and living in Florida, and I had forgotten to call them! It suddenly became very important to me to hear their voices, especially my mother's. I found a phone and dialed their number. Mother answered.

"Mom? Susie had a heart attack!" My voice cracked when I heard my own words; I still couldn't believe it had happened.

"I know, Rick," she said, "Becky and Terri called. How's she doing?" Of course my sisters had called.

"She's not good. She may not live. Can you and Dad come home?"

"We got a flight that gets into Memphis around 10:00 tonight. Becky is picking us up, and we'll come straight to the hospital." That was good. That was real good. Sometimes, no matter how old you are, you still need your mom.

"OK, Mom." I hung up.

Eventually, one by one, family by family, the waiting room emptied out until all that was left were the family members who would stay the night. Sheets, blankets and pillows were brought out, and everyone grabbed a couch or chair. Each family with a loved one in the ICU would stake out a certain area of the waiting room. Your area is respected whether anyone is occupying it or not. We were lucky. We ended up with one of the choice sections - complete with two long couches for easy sleeping. (Right!) The lights went out and relative quiet followed. It was around 10:00, and Susie's sister Jan, her Aunt Jenny and myself stayed the first night. There was no way anyone was going to sleep, and we knew it. I stretched out on the floor and stared at the ceiling. My parents would be there in less than an hour. I settled down to wait.

I probably looked at the clock a hundred times waiting for that hour to pass and the arrival of my parents. I knew they couldn't change things; still, it was comforting somehow, knowing they would soon be there. I saw them through the window in the door and nearly ran to see them. I gave my mother a long hug, very likely the longest of our lives. It was reminiscent of the hug when I left for basic training so many years before. Or another time, when I was ten or eleven, and I left for Boy Scout camp and the first time away from home for more than a night. I knew that as long as I was in her embrace, things were better. Once I let go, however, I would be on my own again.

Dad was emotional - really unusual. Us Jacobs men normally don't get emotional. But, these were not normal circumstances. After a few minutes, they left to go home, and promised to return first thing the next morning. I returned to the dark, lonely waiting room.

I lay back down on the floor. I recall Jan taking my shoes off. I may have actually dozed off once or twice. I do remember the phones ringing a few times during the night. You learned to hate those phones, or it may have been dread. Was it bad news at 2:00 in the morning, or some inconsiderate relative who felt like they just couldn't wait until the next day to see how Aunt Molly was doing? Inevitably, one of the four phones that lined the wall by the door would ring. The closest person would answer, while the rest of the people in the waiting room froze up and prayed their family name wasn't called.

I thought only of Susie that first night. I pictured her in that room by herself, and I longed to be with her. I wanted to hold her hand and talk to her, just assure her I was there, and it was all going to be all right. I wanted to believe it was - I had to believe it was. But, with the reality of the situation, I had no earthly idea what the future held. It was this horrible fear of the unknown that haunted me every hour of every day we were there. It continues even today.

During Susie's stay in the CVICU, there were horrible low points, there were joyous moments. There were times when hope seemed lost and pointless. There were celebrations. There were prayers from soft-spoken Baptist ministers that were sincere and reverent. I'd never forget one prayer from a black minister named Leon who worked at the hospital and was brought to the CVICU by one of the nurses. There is no way God missed this one. It went something like this:

"JEEEsus! HELP this young lady!! DeLIVER her from the pain and anguish she is suffering!! LIFT her up! BEE with her! Have MERcy on her!"

I can't do it justice, but it was wonderful. We went and saw Leon just before we were discharged. I told him his prayer had surely reached God's ears. He was genuinely happy.

I got to know God for the very first time in my life. He and I would talk a lot over the next several weeks. I found He held no grudges over the lack of communication He and I had throughout my life. He made His presence known to me, and He really does answer prayers.

A roller coaster hasn't been built, and could never be built, that would compare to the one I rode over the next week in the ICU. The uphills were agonizingly slow, and the rides down were fast, furious and over all too soon before the next uphill, longer and steeper than the one before, came around. I was in the front car, eyes wide open, terrified of what might be just over the edge or around the corner. I was determined to finish the ride, though. Susie was waiting for me at the end.

Come what may, I would finish the ride.

CHAPTER FIVE:

THE CRITICAL CARE
WAITING ROOM

Inside the four walls of this room more emotions were experienced than anyone can possibly imagine. It's a place you hated to be in because of what it represented.

There are few places in the world that will hold more memories for me than the Critical Care waiting room at Susie's hospital. It was relatively small, maybe 1200 square feet, with nothing more in it than some couches and chairs, tables, a small dining area with a couple of vending machines, a television on one wall and phones on another. Yet, every possible emotion was felt here, both by every member of our family as well as all the other families of patients who were unfortunate enough to be there. There was a common bond among everyone. No one was in this room for happy visits. We all had loved ones who were critically ill. It brought us together in a common cause.

We met families who had been there for several weeks. This was hard to imagine. After only two or three days I could feel the pressure mount. Sleep was nearly non-existent. Appetites dramatically decline. And the lack of both over a period of as little as two or three days takes their toll both physically and mentally. Add to this the tremendous stress of just having to be there and you have some idea what everyone there was going through.

Another stress factor was the limited amount of time we could spend with our loved ones. There were only four times a day that we were allowed to visit, and then for only a half hour per visit. Everyone in the waiting room watched the clock. It became an obsession. It was reminiscent of how time used to drag in school. The hours between visits were mercilessly long, while the half hour spent with Susie flew. I remain grateful to her nurses to this day for allowing me leniency on my visits, especially as she improved somewhat. I repeatedly warned them that I would always ignore the hated announcement, "Attention everyone! Visiting hours are over. Please return to the waiting room and allow your loved ones to get the rest they need and their nurses time to give them the attention vital to their recovery." They had to kick me out. Sometimes they let me stay indefinitely. It really helped between the 12:30 and 5:30 visits - interminably long.

There were things you learned to make the time between visits more productive and easier to take. Naps were difficult - there was just too much noise, too many phone calls and too many visitors. You brought things to read and things to keep you busy. Puzzle books were popular - Find-the-Word or crossword puzzles especially. I roamed a lot. Many times it was easier just to be by myself. I would go outside and find a place to sit. I would people watch, reflect on the future, try to make sense of everything that had happened, or sometimes just to cry and pray. Believe it or not, I grew tired of people coming up to me to tell me of a miracle story that either happened to them or someone they knew. I realized they were trying to cheer me up, but I wasn't interested. I was only interested in Susie's story and of the miracle I hoped she would be. So I would get away, and it got me by. Don't misunderstand - I needed and was grateful for the vast support I got from my family and friends, but sometimes conversation was uncomfortable, and at times, when things looked really grim, I didn't want to talk to anybody. So, I would walk away without telling anyone where I was going. Eventually they got used to it and stopped asking me where I went.

Quarters became a hot item since the dollar slot on the vending machines never worked. We learned to bring several rolls with us and then watch the supply closely. The new arrivals always needed change and we were glad to oblige.

The between meal snacks were plentiful. Someone brought a huge plastic container and we filled it to overflowing within the first day or two. I don't know why, but everyone brought food. Even when Susie had been out of ICU for a couple of weeks, and nothing had been brought to replenish the supply, we still had food. I wonder if those who brought us this bonanza of eats knew how much it was appreciated. It kept us going through the times when eating wasn't a priority, or even a thought.

The waiting room was run by a lady we nicknamed "Helga." She sat in a glass-enclosed room right by the entrance. She was the lady you spoke to for information, and she was also the telephone operator. She ran a tight ship. You didn't break the rules on Helga's watch. I remember vividly one evening when a good friend of mine came to visit and his cell phone rang. He didn't know that cell phones were prohibited on the Cardiac Care floor - the signals may interfere with lifesaving equipment. He made a bigger mistake when he answered it. The voice over the loudspeaker was immediate, loud and all business:

"THE USE OF CELL PHONES ON THIS FLOOR IS STRICTLY PROHIBITED! THERE ARE EQUIPMENT IN PATIENTS ROOMS WHICH COULD MALFUNCTION. PLEASE TURN OFF ALL CELL PHONES IMMEDIATELY!"

He did, sheepishly, like he just got caught cheating on a test. I thought at the time that the way she handled it was a tad extreme, but she was just doing her job, and with Susie hooked up to some of that equipment I'd rather the phones stay turned off as well.

For the first two nights the waiting room was also my bedroom. At first, I couldn't stand the thought of leaving the hospital for any more time than to take a shower and change. The third night, though, changed my mind. I hadn't planned on it until I settled down to try and get some sleep. I had gotten maybe four hours total in the previous two nights, and I was exhausted. I was drained. I closed my eyes, and then they started. Two people in a section next to ours decided that 11:00 p.m. was talk time. They didn't sit next to each other and whisper; they were 15 feet apart and talking in normal conversational volume. The lights were out, everyone in the room was lying down on pillows and covered in blankets; the TV was off, yet these weren't enough clues for them to figure that maybe it was time to shut up. I wanted to walk over to them and say something, but I didn't. I got up, told Jan where I was going, then went home and got three or four hours of solid sleep in my own bed. It was the first real sleep I had been able to get since the ordeal began, and it refreshed me. It was good to see my kids outside of the hospital as well. From then on I spent nights at home with my children.

Everyone knew everyone there and the condition of their loved one. Susie especially, both in the waiting room and in the CVICU, because of her young age and the huge family support she maintained throughout her hospital stay. The fact that she had young children also contributed to her recognition - especially with the nurses. Most of their patients had grand-children, or even great grandchildren, our kid's ages. A lot of the nurses had young children as well. The fact that Susie was so young and had so much to live for may have made those who cared for her work just a little bit harder. Maybe not, but it didn't hurt. I talked to one of Susie's nurses after she was discharged, and she admitted she had become attached to her and to our family. She said it had never happened before. It made Susie cry.

In a classic case of "where were you when...?" I was in the critical care waiting room when the news of the terrorist attacks in New York and Washington first came on television. This happened only six days after Susie's heart attack and she remained very critical on the morning of September 11. I noticed the waiting room was suddenly very quiet, and that everyone was looking at the TV. When I say quiet, I mean pin drop quiet. Very strange. I looked at the television screen and saw what was happening. I found that I just didn't care. I felt bad about it later, but at the time the only thing in the world I cared about lay on the edge of death down the hall. I think perhaps as well that, psychologically, I couldn't handle more bad news.

The critical care waiting room was a place where I spent the better part of eight days. From Wednesday afternoon,

September 5, until late Thursday night, September 13. I worried, cried, prayed, ate, slept, visited, worried and prayed. I saw people I hadn't seen in years. Susie had so many visitors that we filled five legal pad pages with names. I had intentions to send thank you cards to all of them.

I shared stories of Susie and our life with others, and they shared likewise stories of their loved ones with me. Inside the four walls of that room more emotions were experienced than anyone can possibly imagine. It's a place you hated to be in because of what it represented. Those eight days were an eternity. I couldn't imagine being there longer.

I spent many hours with my family and with Susie's family in this room. More than I had spent in a long, long time. Susie and I had worked 70-80 hours a week for the last year and a half with our new business. The time off we were suddenly taking had seemed impossible before her illness. A lot of things would change over the next several weeks. Many events would occur that would test my sanity and my ability to cope. I reflect back over the time I spent in the critical care waiting room sometimes - those eight days seemed like eight years - and I marvel at how well we managed. When you consider how our world literally changed in the blink of an eye, it now seems incredible we were somehow able to take things an hour at a time. We lived from visit to visit. We waited for each of Susie's doctors to give us the updates of her condition, her prognosis and the plans for her treatment. We waited to hear our name called from Helga for the phone calls that came so frequently. Mostly, though, we waited for the news that Susie would be released to the next level of care. There were only two ways to be released from the ICU. One way was to get better.

The other way wasn't an option.

CHAPTER SIX:

THE SCARE

An alarm bell went off. But it was louder and more ominous than any I had heard before. Scott was instantly on it. He moved over to Susie and said, "Rick, you need to leave the room!"

Somehow, I made it through the first night of Susie's hospital stay. More importantly, so did Susie.

There were no middle of the night calls. I figured no news was good news. I believe I actually dozed off once or twice that first night. I know I was surprised to see that it was nearly 5 a.m. when I finally got up. Jan was still asleep. There was a coffee maker in the kitchen area of the waiting room so I made my way there. I figured out how to make a fresh pot and did so as quietly as possible so as not to disturb anyone else who may be sleeping. There is no way of knowing how much coffee I drank over the next several days in that ICU waiting room. There would be pretty much non-stop java drinking until lunch and sometimes beyond. Unusual for me - I normally drank two cups in the morning and sometimes three on Sundays.

While the coffee brewed, I walked over to the phones and dialed the CVICU direct number. As usual someone answered after the first ring. I asked for Scott.

"This is Scott."

"Scott, this is Rick Jacobs. Susie's husband. How's she doing?" The ever-present ache in my stomach intensified, as it always did whenever I was getting ready to find out news that could be bad. As I explained before, until I knew for sure, Susie was well. I hope that makes sense. In other words, she wouldn't die until someone told me she died. She would have had a good night right up until Scott told me she had a bad night. It makes sense to me, anyway.

"There's not much change, Rick. We're watching her very closely. Her heartbeat right now is really irregular and we're concerned about that. We've called the cardiologist on call in, and we'll see what she says."

"Can I come see her?" *Please, please, please!*

He hesitated. "OK, come on, but just you and only for a minute."

There is a long hallway from the elevators to the entrance of the CVICU. Probably a hundred feet or more. Just in front of the double doors and to the right on the wall was a large round silver push button. Sometimes, if you were lucky, you could push it and the doors would open. This usually didn't happen when visiting hours weren't in effect. If you weren't lucky, you were forced to press the intercom button and wait for a nurse to open the doors from the desk inside. I had to use the intercom.

"Yes? Can I help you?"

I was out of breath from the run from the waiting room. "This is Rick Jacobs. Scott said I could come see Susie." There was a few seconds of waiting, then the doors opened. I walked in and turned the corner to Susie's room. Scott was in there with her, preparing a shot. I looked at Susie and again my heart sank. Her eyes were closed. She seemed peaceful enough. There was a feeding tube in her nose. The breathing tube was still down her throat. I stood there, more or less frozen. I wanted to scoop her up, take her out of there, and then go home and pretend nothing had happened. I was supposed to be at work right now. She was supposed to get up in a couple of hours, get the kids off to school then come to work like always. How could things change so dramatically and so quickly? How was it possible that my wife, so young and so needed, could have a heart attack and walk such a thin line between life and death?

Scott seemed to read my mind. "We're watching her real close, Rick." He laid a hand on my shoulder. I just stared at her. "See the heart monitor up there?" He pointed to a screen above her head. "These are what concerns us right now." He showed me what he meant. In very crude layman's terms, there were peaks that were good. Her heart was getting a good, strong signal to beat, but they were very irregular, with what looked like small, hilly lines in between. Alarms were continually going off. "These alarm bells you hear tell us every time her heartbeat is missing for a certain amount of time. It hasn't stopped completely since yesterday, but we're keeping a close eye on her."

I was stunned. There would be a peak, several of the small hills, a peak, then an alarm. Scott pressed a button, and the alarm bell stopped. It was terrible.

"Will she be alright?" I could barely whisper the words. My mind couldn't grasp this. How could her heart attack have been that severe? Was there so much damage that she may need a heart transplant? Was there still a possibility of another attack?

"It's just too soon to know, Rick. The first 48 hours are critical. Your cardiologist can tell you more. Her name is Dr. Simonson." I told him that I wished that one of our good customers, Dr. Joe Weinstein, was taking care of her. He said, "Rick, I work for Dr. Weinstein!"

I looked at him. Suddenly I wanted Dr. Weinstein to take care of Susie. I had to have him. I felt a sense of calm knowing that someone who knew us, and knew us well, would be calling the shots. There was no debate. "Can he be our doctor?"

"Yes, he can. All you have to do is request him."

"Then do it. We request him. Can you take care of it for us?"

"I can do the paperwork. You have to talk to Dr. Simonson and tell her personally that she is off the case. She won't be happy."

I didn't care. I had to have Dr. Weinstein. I then walked over to Susie; there were so many IV lines. I carefully took her hand; it was warm, and that was comforting somehow. I guessed because cold is synonymous with death, warmth with life. I leaned over to her and kissed her cheek. I whispered in her ear, "Susie, can you hear me?" There was no response.

"Susie, honey, I don't know if you can hear me or not, but I'm right here. I'm right beside you and I always will be. We're going to get through this, you hear me? You're going to be OK." My voice cracked as I finished speaking, and a tear fell on her ear. I wiped it off with my hand. I kissed her again and stepped back. I looked at Scott. "Scott," I said, "how soon will we know? When…?" I couldn't say it. He knew what I was asking.

"Time will tell, Rick. We have the best doctors in the world here; I do know that. I'll tell you something I've learned in seven years of nursing. Prayer works. I've seen miracles that could only be attributed to prayer."

I will admit that, up until that very moment, my faith had been minimum at best. I knew God existed - I just didn't know what He really had to do with the world or with my own life. I knew how blessed I had been, at least up until the day before. I had four wonderful children, all in good health. I had my own health. I had a wonderful wife who could only be described as an angel. I had joined the Catholic church only a few months before, more than anything to make my Susie happy. I had no regrets. I loved going to church as a family and it thrilled Susie. It was at that moment I began talking to God. Because it was at that exact moment that an alarm went off. It was louder and more ominous than any I had heard before.

Scott was instantly on it. He moved over to Susie, instantly analyzed the alarm, and said, "Rick, you need to leave the room!" I walked out in a daze. Two or three other nurses passed me on their way in and one of them closed the curtain around her bed and blocked my view. I don't know what happened. I don't know what they had to do to her. I never asked. I just know that I prayed. "Please, God, don't take her from me. Not yet." Over and over. I refused to leave the ICU until I knew. "God, I need her. I can't do this without her. She has four kids who need her. Please, God, she's too young." Over and over and over. Finally, they came out. Scott came over to me. "She's OK, Rick, just a little scare."

I sat down in a chair, buried my hands in my face, and cried. Scott put his arms on my shoulders and said, "Listen, man, go home and take a shower. Change clothes. Make sure your kids are OK." I hadn't even thought of them. Suddenly I needed to see them. I nodded to him, composed myself and got up. "It's going to be a long road, Rick. Prepare yourself for it. You've got to take care of yourself or you won't make it. You need food and sleep. Your kids are going to need you now more than ever." I nodded again, thanked him, and left.

This was Scott, and really all of the nurses that I would get to know. Almost without exception, they were as compassionate to my family and me as they were to Susie. I have never known people like them. I will probably say this over and over throughout this book, but it bears repeating. They don't make enough money. They deserve all the accolades I can give and more. Because of them, Susie survived and so did I. If I live to be 90, their faces and their way above and beyond actions will remain as vivid to me as they are at this moment.

I took Scott's advice and drove home. Outside, the air was hot and humid as it always is in Memphis in early September. I managed to find my car - I don't know who drove it to the hospital the previous afternoon. I barely remember someone telling me that it was in the parking lot. I got in, put the key in the ignition and turned it. The radio was on, and I immediately turned it off. In the ensuing silence, I sat in reflection. I looked outside through the front windshield. There were a few cars on the road in front of the hospital in the dark, early morning hour. I envied them. They were either going to work or coming from it. They hadn't a care in the world, even if they didn't know it. I made my way out of the lot and onto the road. Our home was only a couple of miles from the hospital. I was glad of that. I was driving, immersed in thought, when suddenly a very loud truck flew around me and swerved directly back in front of me. He was making sure I knew he was mad. I was confused, until I looked down and saw I was doing less than 30 miles per hour. I actually said out loud, "Buddy, if your biggest problem right now is me slowing you down, you don't know how fortunate you are." I sped up a little.

I got home and walked in. I threw my car keys on the kitchen table and walked into the living room. The kids were spread out on couches and chairs, none of them wanting to sleep in their rooms. Being close to each other was important, I guess. They were moving, having heard me come in. They asked how Mom was, and I briefly told them what I knew. I left out the scary alarm. I told them to go back to sleep and that I was going to shower and change. They asked if they could miss school and go back to the hospital with me. How could I say no? I told them I would be ready in half an hour.

The bedroom was tough on me. I knew it would be. Her side of the bed. Her pictures all over the room. Her makeup mirror in the bathroom. Her perfumes, soaps and all that was exclusively hers were everywhere. How long, I wondered, would it be before she would be home again? *Would* she be home again? I tried to imagine what I would do without her. It was too horrible to even consider. I took my shower, and went through the motions of shaving and getting dressed in total silence.

I turned off the bathroom light and walked back out into the bedroom. I half-expected to see Susie in bed, her body under the blankets, her face and hair on her pillow, sound asleep. But the bed was empty. She was in a different bed now, and would be for a while. I was alone. I had family and friends in abundance who would be there for me. And yet, I was intolerably alone. The realization of what had happened began to take shape, especially now, in the familiar surroundings of our home. I was here and Susie wasn't. My own heart began to race, and my breaths became rapid and loud. I sat down and fought the urge to cry. My kids couldn't see me this way. I had to be strong. I didn't want to scare them.

I regrouped and gathered everyone together. I tried to explain that Mom was very sick and would be in the hospital for quite a while. With our six-year-old in the room I left out the heart attack part. They were fine. In fact, they were amazing. This made it so much easier on me.

Everyone has heard, "Today is the first day of the rest of your life." That is what the first full day after Susie's heart attack really was. Our lives changed dramatically, instantly and without warning. What happens to others happened to us. The rest of our lives, we found, do not necessarily go on according to plans we make. Plans can change. Plans do change. Our world of dry-cleaning, shirts and smoke-damaged clothing, once so important, became meaningless, replaced by hospitals, doctors, nurses, unimaginable fear and loneliness.

This would all start today. Day one of the rest of our lives.

CHAPTER SEVEN:

THE SECOND TIME

I remember thinking that people usually die after suffering massive heart attacks.

The first full day of Susie's hospital stay was pretty much non-stop worry, confusion and visitors. In that order. We were all intensely worried about Susie, that's goes without saying, but I had other important things to consider that I had gnawing at me even this early on. I had four children, and my youngest, Scotty, had just started kindergarten this year. He boarded the bus on this morning just like every other morning. He was so proud to be big enough to ride that bus to school and back every day. We knew it was best to keep his routine going. My other three kids, Sean, 11, Ricky, Jr., 15, and Lisa, 18, were all at the hospital. They all knew how serious their mom was. There was no way to keep her condition from them. My other worry was our business. My brother-in-law, Lee, was operating the store for me until I could get back. Still, as gracious as that was, I couldn't help but be anxious about it. That store was like a fifth child to Susie and me. We watched it grow and develop into a prosperous endeavor. A lot of sweat, tears and toil went into it. But at the time there was nothing I could or would do about it. It simply had to survive until I or, hopefully, we could return.

Then there was the confusion. Susie was young, and not the least bit overweight. There was no family history of this sort of heart disease. She did smoke - about a pack a day for the last 15 years or so. There were long, long hours at work and the stress that comes with opening and going through the growing pains of a new business. It was hell for the first year. We lost a lot of sleep. While all of these factors - smoking, stress, fatigue - are obvious contributors to heart attacks, we never imagined it could happen at such a young age.

It was also beginning to get much better. The last six months or so we were starting to enjoy the fruits of our labor. She had just bought a nearly new Ford Excursion - the biggest, baddest SUV that Ford makes. She bought it by herself. In fact, when she called me and said she wanted it, I didn't know what it was. I just told her that if she liked it, get it. I almost fainted when she drove up in it. I planned to get a license plate that said "Susie's Ark." How she loved that car. I was so proud that we were able to get it.

Another way that we knew we were beginning to really do well is that, literally the day before her heart attack, we looked at a new house. It was love at first sight. All of her life, Susie wanted a front porch that ran the whole length of the front of her house. This place had it. It was incredible. We looked at the inside and noticed that none of the carpeting, paint, tile or anything else had been installed so Susie could pick all of this. The kitchen was huge - it was perfect. Nearly perfect, anyway. She would have loved to have had one more bedroom, and then it really would have been. But, with that front porch, she didn't care. We even took all the kids over that night and let them run all through the empty rooms. I remember thinking, man, we did it. All the hard work finally paid off. First an Excursion and now a new house. I was so thrilled for Susie. I'd live in a double wide with her and be happy - I truly didn't care. But it was a real pleasure to be able to do this for her. I remember one day right after we had gotten the SUV talking to my mother. She asked why we had bought such a big car. I told her because Susie wanted it. I said this to her then, and this is an exact quote:

"Mother, I've never seen her so happy, and what else have I got to do, really, except make her happy?"

I don't tell this story to make myself look like super husband. I included it only because I was so very glad to have said it. It gave me comfort in the long, tough days ahead.

I was also confused on what was happening now and what would happen in the days ahead. Medically speaking especially. I didn't know the difference between a cardiogram and echogram - two terms I have learned only since her heart attack. This was an issue that I didn't think about until I would talk about Susie with one of her many doctors. Especially in the first few days. My mind was already in torment - I could barely concentrate on where I was. I would talk to someone, and by the time I got back to the waiting room and tried to relate what had just been said to some very anxious family members, I had no idea what I had just been told. Thank God for Susie's Aunt Jenny. She was a registered nurse, and had been the head nurse at an emergency room for 15 years. She could talk with the doctors and nurses, ask the right questions, inquire about current and future treatments, then translate into layman's terms to the rest of us. She was truly a blessing. It gave us a lot of comfort during some tough times. She took a lot of vacation days to spend time with us. I will be forever grateful for her comforting presence and her ever-upbeat demeanor. She would also take a role in Susie's care throughout her hospital stay.

And of course, there were lots of visitors. I'll never forget one time, years ago, Susie had said to me that she didn't have any friends. I said, "What are you talking about, Susie, you have lots of friends."

"No I don't, Rick. I don't have anyone that's like a real friend. Name somebody." I tried. Everyone I came up with was a family member, and that didn't count, really. Guys are lucky. We play golf after work, we make friends through business. I play a trombone and know lots of people from that. I bet I have 100 people I could call my friend. But, at that time, Susie didn't. Mothers have their children to take care of and that becomes a full time job. She had lots of friends before kids. But once our kids, and the kids of all her friends, got old enough for school and, especially, sports, the hours once spent with close friends were gone. She took the roll of homework checker, project helper, taxi, and, without realizing it, our kids became her life. All this was balanced with working at our cleaners, housework and cooking. I gave her time to do this, so golf was justified in my mind, as well as all of the other fun things I did. But the realization was good for me. I helped out more.

The reason I mention this, is that if she could have seen all of the people who came to see her and wanted her well, she would never make that statement again. We all prayed diligently that she would survive to read all the names we wrote in that legal pad. Every visitor signed in, and we even wrote down the names of those who called and were unable to be there in person. It was amazing. Many times, it was overwhelming.

It was around mid-morning on that first day when we heard Helga's voice come over the loudspeaker and announce, "Jacobs family!" Eventually I got used to hearing my name, but at that early stage of things I would spring out of the seat like it had caught fire, then cover the distance to the phones without even realizing I had gotten up. Breathlessly, I said, "This is Rick Jacobs. "

"Mr. Jacobs, can you come to the ICU? Dr. Weinstein is here to see you." I told her I would be right there and hung up. I remember staring at the wall for just a second, catching my breath. This is it, I thought. Now, we would know. I turned around, and as I expected, everyone was anxiously looking at me. I motioned for Jenny to come over to me. She did, and I explained to her that Susie's cardiologist was waiting for me. I asked her if she'd go with me. Of course, she wanted to be there. She went back to the rest of the family and told them where we were going, and then we were on our way.

That same old fear of the unknown enveloped me once again. What I didn't know couldn't yet hurt me. Now, though, I wanted to know - I *had* to know. I didn't remember walking to the ICU. All of a sudden we were there and I was shaking his hand and introducing him to Jenny. I gave him her credentials. They shook hands. I'll never forget his first words to me after that.

"Rick, Susie had a massive heart attack. I mean, it was a doozy."

I absorbed what he said. A massive heart attack! I remember thinking that people usually die after suffering massive heart attacks. You read news stories, "He suffered a massive heart attack *and died*" all the time. It was the first time that anyone had said this to me. The reality of it then hit me for the first time, the stone cold reality that was inescapable, of what had happened to my wife.

I mumbled, "Well, what do we do? Will she be OK?"

He actually smiled. "Oh, yeah! I can fix it. I got the tools to do it." He was wonderfully cocky. He was so sure of himself I felt immediately relieved. He then said, "I'm really glad you decided to put me as Susie's doctor. I don't want to brag, but you got the best! OK?" He held out his hand and I shook it. Sometimes all you need to make you feel good is a handshake that is backed up with a smile that says, don't worry, I got it covered! This is how I felt at that moment. He and Jenny talked about what was being done at that time, and what was planned for the future, but I wasn't listening. I'd get it later. I was looking into Susie's room, trying to get a glimpse of her, when Scott called my name. He was at the nurse's station with a phone in his hand. I went over to him.

"Here you go, Rick," he said, covering one end of the phone with his palm. "It's Dr. Simonson, and as I said, she's not happy." I remembered Scott telling me I would have to personally take her off Susie's case. I had no problem doing so. I remembered meeting her when I saw pictures of Susie's heart before and after the stent implants. She was young, much younger than I would expect a cardiologist to be, but extremely efficient and nice to me. I liked her, but I knew Dr. Weinstein.

"Dr. Simonson? This is Rick Jacobs, Susie's husband."

"Yes, Rick, I understand you're taking me off as her doctor?"

"Yeah, Doc, I am. I want Dr. Weinstein to take her now."

"Why, Rick? I did a good job on her yesterday." She was upset.

"I know you did, and I'm eternally grateful. It's just that I know Dr. Weinstein. I know him really well. It's nothing personal."

"Why didn't you ask for him yesterday?"

She had to be kidding! "Doc, I wasn't thinking exactly

straight about anything yesterday. I didn't care who helped her, as long as she got some help."

"OK, but listen, Rick. What I did for your wife yesterday was exactly right. I don't want to hear about anything sometime down the road."

So that was it! She was worried about a malpractice lawsuit or something to that effect. "Doc, that is the least of your worries. It simply won't happen. You saved her life, and I am well aware of that."

That softened her up. "OK, Rick, I understand. I hope your wife gets better."

So did I.

I hung up and went back to Jenny. We had the same idea. Our arms went up at the same time and we hugged each other hard. There was so much relief. He could fix her heart! She would be OK! Ever the realist, she let me know the road to recovery would be long. "It won't be overnight, Rick. Be prepared for a long hospital stay."

I nodded, wiping my eyes with my sleeves. "Let's go give everyone the good news."

And we did. Jenny did most of the talking, going over what Dr. Weinstein had told us, then adding what she knew would be happening based on her years of experience. There were tears and hugs all around as we shared the news of her now eventual recovery. At that moment, I didn't care how long it would take. We had time - she was only 39! And Dr. Weinstein wasn't pretty sure he could fix her, he was damn sure he could do it! She would live, and we would eventually go home and continue on with our lives with no more than a speed bump in the road. A mere hiccup! I felt good, and then realized I was incredibly hungry. I don't know who brought food, but I had a good lunch.

The remainder of the day was a blur. I made all the kids go home after the last visitation, leaving Jan, Jenny and myself to stay the night. We were pretty happy, considering it had only been about 36 hours since Susie's heart attack. But she would recover, no doubt about it. And there was no doubt about it, right up until a nurse from the ICU came into the waiting room sometime that night, that same Thursday night, and woke us.

"Mr. Jacobs," she said, "I have to tell you that your wife's heart stopped again, just a little while ago."

The words hit me like a ton of bricks. There was nothing she could have said that would have shocked me more. She told me they were able to immediately start it beating. With no more than a thump to her chest, it began beating completely on its own. There had been no problems since, but I was absolutely crushed. This was the roller coaster I rode throughout her recovery. From euphoria to despair in the blink of an eye.

"What do you mean it stopped?" I asked. "It just stopped? Is this normal? Could it happen again? Is there still a chance that Susie may still die? Aren't we out of the woods? Isn't this what Dr. Weinstein basically said, that he could fix her heart, and she would be OK?" It was as if I was betrayed over a broken promise. I had made the mistake of letting my guard down.

The nurse was sympathetic, and I was assured they were watching her very closely. It was good that her heart began beating so easily. Susie was still not out of danger. Her nurse didn't believe, however, that any more damage to her heart occurred since it had stopped for such a brief period of time. They were just telling me this out of procedure. When something happens to a patient like this, they have to tell the immediate family. She said, "Try not to worry. I will let you know immediately if anything happens. Try and get some sleep."

Try and get some sleep? She had to know that was now an impossibility. Her heart had stopped *again!* Wasn't once enough? This never occurred to me, after meeting with Dr. Weinstein, that it was remotely possible that it could happen. I sat in stunned silence, staring at nothing, all three of us too crushed to speak to one another. It was too late to call anybody. I don't know how long I sat there before I lay down on the floor again. I had brought Susie's pillow to the hospital, and I reached over, pulled it to me, and bear hugged it. It was at least partly Susie, and I held on to it for dear life. I closed my eyes and pictured her laying alone in her bed down the hall. I pictured her heart in her body. What I saw was a damaged organ, barely beating, shreds of tissue hanging off. Her heart would beat, shudder, beat, then shudder. Susie would convulse over and over, and I begged her, in my mind, to hang on. I hoped that our minds were as one, and I pleaded with her again and again to hang on and come back home with me. It was a horrible, horrible night.

I finally got up, sleep totally non-existent, and looked at the clock. It was nearly 5:00. I made some coffee and waited for it to brew. My mind was numb - clear thoughts were impossible. I poured some coffee and somehow staggered to my car. I have no idea how, I don't remember anything about the drive, but I suddenly found myself parked behind our cleaners. The back door was open, and I knew my brother-in-law was already there getting ready for the day. I got out of the car and went inside.

Lee saw me. "Rick? What are you doing here?"

I don't know what I said. I mumbled something. I looked around the back, at the presses, the clothes waiting to be cleaned and pressed, and it meant nothing to me. It was as if I had never been there before. I made my way to the front of the store. Lee followed me without a word.

I found myself in the front office. To my left was our private office. This is where her heart attack had happened. I walked in.

I looked around and saw her adding machine that she added the day's tickets on. Her computer was right beside it, where she entered daily totals, deposits, payroll and played games. There were notes with her handwriting taped and tacked everywhere. There were pictures on the wall from various stages of our opening and operations, and she was in them. Then I looked down on the floor where it all happened. I relived it. Then I lost it.

The tears and sobs came from nowhere. I sat down on one of the office chairs and cried like a baby. Poor Lee was right behind me, and he didn't know what to do. He tried laying a hand on my shoulder and saying something, but I didn't understand him. He withdrew the hand, and then stood there in case I did need him. I have no idea how long I cried. I do know that, in 45 years of life, it was the most outpouring of emotion I had ever done, at least that I could remember.

I finally got up, feeling better. It had helped. It needed to come out. Lee asked me if I was OK, and I told him yeah, and that I had to go get Scotty on the bus. He asked me how Susie was, and I told him there was no change. I went home, showered, shaved, and got Scotty on his school bus. I told the kids nothing about the night before. They didn't need to know.

I had spent two nights with little or no sleep, yet I wasn't sleepy. I had little to eat, but I wasn't hungry. I had spent the last two days constantly surrounded by family, friends, doctors and nurses. And yet, none of them mattered. The only one who could possibly give me any comfort, at that moment in my life, was helpless to do so. It seemed increasingly likely as well that she may never again.

This was a sobering reflection; one that I never imagined I would have to consider so early in our lives. I removed it from my mind, refusing to lose hope this early. Once again, I willed our minds together.

"Don't you dare leave me, Susie," I whispered, "Don't you dare!"

CHAPTER EIGHT:

THE ROLLER COASTER

She looked at Jenny, and of course Jenny knew. "Rick, her heart was stopped for a long time. There could be some brain damage."

There was chapel on the first floor of the hospital. It was a small room, quiet and reassuring. When I parked my car on Friday morning, I knew this would be the first place I would go. I was new at this, talking to God. I would pray at church when I went with the family at Sunday morning mass. I would thank Him for the many blessings He had bestowed on my family. The new business was doing well, we all had our health and I was grateful. I told Him this every Sunday. But this was a whole new ballgame. I would now ask Him to help Susie stay alive.

I located the room after much searching and finally asking someone where it was. I found myself inside the chapel, alone, kneeling at the alter and staring at the crucifix on the wall in front of me. I didn't close my eyes. I prayed out loud, in a whispered voice that had never been so reverent before this moment.

"God," I prayed, "it's me. I know we haven't talked much before, but I'm desperate. You know where Susie is, and You know how sick she is. Please let her stay, God. You've got enough angels, but she's all I have. Help her, God, please help her. I can't do this alone. I can't take much more. I don't know how much You expect from me, but if she gets better I'll be there for her and for You. That's a promise. Please God, let her live."

That's as close to verbatim as I can remember. I remember it well because I would say those same words often over the next few weeks. Every time I went to church. Every time I closed my eyes in bed. Especially in bed. I would reach over where Susie was supposed to be and lay my hand on the cold, empty sheet. Then I would ask God, again, to one night let her be there again. I would ask Him driving to and from the hospital. And I would ask Him when I was alone with her in the ICU. I prayed a lot in that room. It was one of the very few things I could do for her.

In the hospital chapel on that Friday morning, though, that

was really the first time that I talked *to* Him. One on one, out loud. And when I was done, I felt a little better somehow. I felt He heard me and was listening. I was sure that we had communicated, God and me. And we still do. I talk to Him a lot these days.

The 8:30 visit came around and I didn't know what to expect. I had already talked to Susie's nurse more than once that morning. Her heart had not stopped during the night other than the one time. It was beating very irregularly, however, and it still was when I entered her room. I called her name, as did everyone who came in to see her, but there was nothing. I avoided looking at the heart monitor. There were far too few peaks and too many hills. The alarm bells were constant.

The bed guards were always up whenever we visited her in the ICU. One of the first things I always did when I first entered was lower two of them on her left side. She sure wasn't going anywhere. There was a chair on that side of her bed that I always pulled up close, and I would sit there and hold her hand, and talk to her. Sometimes I would lay my head on her. Everyone has heard stories of people in comatose conditions who, once they woke up, would state emphatically that they remembered hearing their loved ones speaking to them. I always assumed Susie heard every word I said. I made sure I didn't make promises I couldn't keep.

The first visit of the morning came and went. They let me stay a few minutes longer. It was always wonderful being alone with her. I could say things that I couldn't otherwise. I would talk about the plans that we had for the future. I would talk about the kids and our business. I especially talked about little Scotty. He was our baby, even though he was six, and I thought he was our best bet to bring her back. I would put Vaseline on her lips, swab her forehead with a cold rag, and comb her hair - whatever I could think of to make her comfortable. There was always this incredibly helpless feeling.

The first time I talked to a neurologist was on this Friday morning. Her name was Dr. Pulan. She was of Middle Eastern descent and had a thick accent that was hard to understand at times. I had not considered the possibility of brain damage before then. I was so involved with her physical well-being that her mental condition wasn't even a concern. I got a call in the waiting room from Dr. Pulan, and once again Jenny and myself went down the long hall. Dr. Pulan had jet-black hair, including her eyebrows, and the wire rim glasses she wore added to her obvious intelligence. She was young, and she greeted us just outside of Susie's room. She held out her hand to both of us.

"Hi, I'm Dr. Pulan. It's nice to meet you. Are you Mr. Jacobs? " She took my hand, and I nodded. I introduced her to Jenny. She moved immediately on to Susie.

"Mr. Jacobs, your wife was given an EEG this morning. This is a test that measures brain activity. The test this morning showed good brain activity."

I was glad to hear it, of course, but I didn't understand why she needed the test. "Why would we need to know that? Why wouldn't her brain be OK?"

She looked at Jenny, and of course Jenny knew. "Rick, her heart was stopped for a long time. There could be some brain damage."

I hadn't thought of this. My God, what next? Dr. Pulan asked me, "Mr. Jacobs, how long do you think it was between the time her heart stopped and when the paramedics arrived?"

I had to think. It seemed like forever. "Three or four minutes, I guess."

Her eyes darted to Jenny and then back to me. "Was there CPR given on the scene? Before the paramedics got there?"

"I gave her mouth-to-mouth."

"What about chest pumping to get blood flowing?"

I tried to remember. It seemed one of our customers tried this. I didn't see how it could have been very effective. "If we did, I don't think it worked very well." I began to get a bad feeling about where this was going. "You said the test this morning showed good activity. That won't change, will it?"

"Mr. Jacobs, your wife's brain was without blood flow for several minutes. The brain can withstand no oxygen without problem for two or three minutes at the most. From three to four minutes there will be some damage. Longer than four minutes can be catastrophic."

I let that sink in. Catastrophic brain damage? I thought back to when it happened. No matter how I tried to remember, it had to be longer than four minutes from the time we knew there was no pulse until the paramedics arrived. It had to be. And even after that, they shocked her at least three or four times until they got a pulse. How long was that? Brain damage. It was a real possibility.

"When will we know?"

"The EEG, again, showed good brain activity at this time. This is not necessarily brain function, but it is still good news in as much that it means there is potential for some recovery. Now..."

I stopped her. "Some recovery? Dr. Pulan, are you saying that Susie will have at least *some* brain damage?"

She nodded. "I think there is no question she will have some brain damage. The question is how much and where it will be. Right now, her brain is swelling from the trauma it suffered. Unfortunately, there is no room for the brain to swell. It will expand against the cranium for five days or so, and then it will shrink back down gradually for another five days. It is very possible additional damage will occur at this time. We will have to wait until then."

Jenny spoke up. "What about ordering an MRI, Doctor?"

Dr. Pulan shook her head. "We have to wait at least six weeks before we can do an MRI because of the stents in her heart. The magnets of the MRI could dislodge the stents. We have to allow them time to grow into the surrounding tissue."

I tried to understand what was being said to me. Even if Susie survived her heart attack, she could be hurt mentally. "What can you do for her?"

The one thing I would learn about Dr. Pulan is that her tone of voice and expression never changed. She was clinical, professional. She never smiled, she never frowned. "The brain is the one organ of the body that cannot recover. Every other organ will regenerate itself, but the brain cannot. When brain cells die, they are not replaced with new cells. What I will do now is give her Dilantin to prevent seizures. Seizures are a real possibility right now and they can be very detrimental. This drug will anesthetize her brain and decrease dramatically the risk of seizure."

Jenny knew about this drug. "Doctor, won't the Dilantin slow her neurological progress?"

"It could, but seizures are very dangerous and could cause many problems. We must avoid seizures." She looked back at me. "That's all we can do for her right now, Mr. Jacobs. Time will tell."

Jenny and I walked back to the waiting room and tried to tell everyone what we had just been told. I let her do most of the talking. I had gotten to the point by now where I kept to myself a lot when I was in the waiting room. I avoided all talk about Susie's condition and prognosis. I would engage in conversation, especially when new visitors would arrive or I would get a phone call. Mostly, though, I would try to remain alone with my own thoughts and hopes. It's funny, but as I said before, I got really tired of everyone offering me so much hope for the future. I got to where I hated all the stories of those who were worse off than Susie, then miraculously rising up and walking out of the hospital good as new. None of the nurses ever told me a story like that. How many stories could be told of those similar to Susie's condition who didn't get up and walk away? It's like hearing about so and so who went to the casino and hit it big. Sure, it could happen, but far and away more people lost everything they had. I refused, at this point, to get my hopes up. I tried to remain neutral. I would let God do His will. It was all I could do.

I called the ICU a few minutes before the next visiting time and asked if I could cheat. The nurse I spoke to was extremely cheerful. "Rick," she said, "I was just getting ready to call you. Come on back right now. She's awake!"

I dropped the phone and flew through the doors. I literally ran all the way to the ICU. I pressed the intercom button, and the doors opened immediately. I walked around the corner and into her room. There were three nurses there surrounding her bed. They were all smiles. One of them motioned for me to get closer. I walked up to Susie's bed. She looked over at me, her eyes wide open. Then she did something I'll never forget.

She smiled at me!

I nearly lost it. An overwhelming sense of relief washed over me and it was all I could do to remain standing. It was as if the whole world had just been pushed off my shoulders and I was suddenly so light that I thought I might just float away. I looked into her eyes. She was looking right at me. I picked her hand up and kissed it. "Susie? Can you hear me?"

She couldn't say anything, of course - that horrible breathing tube was still in her mouth. But she smiled again! I put my face next to hers, kissed her cheek, and whispered "I love you" into her ear. Then I cried on her shoulder. I couldn't let her see me cry, but I did. After thirty seconds or so, I began to hear familiar voices behind me. I had forgotten about it being visiting time. All the family saw me do was run out the door. I imagined they had to be worried sick! I gathered myself and turned to greet them. "Guys," I said, "Come and see this!"

There must have been ten or fifteen people in her room, all gathered around her bed. Everyone had come at once. They were so worried she had taken a turn for the worse. What happened next can only be described as a one-woman show, starring Susie. I had taken my usual spot on her left and held her hand. Susie looked around the room, and as she saw those she knew and loved, she would smile at them. With every smile, a cheer rose up from everybody. Laughing, cheering and tears were everywhere. The most exciting part of all of this was that there was real communication between Susie and the rest of us. She couldn't talk, of course, but she responded to our questions with blinking. Once, when we asked her if she was ready to go to the casinos, she answered with rapid and numerous blinks, as if to say, "Oh, *hell* yeah!" There was no question whatsoever she understood, and she even showed us a sense of humor, despite her obvious discomfort.

You could tell she hated the breathing tube. She gagged on it constantly. We were told this was good. Her gag reflex was alive and well and this was vital. Eventually she would be able to eat on her own. (It would never stop being strange to me, hearing that Susie would be able to do things again that were so elementary. She would be able to *eat* again. She would be able to *breathe* again. Hopefully she would be able to *feed herself* again. Over the next few weeks, this would become commonplace.)

Scott was in the background, but now he came to her bed. "Watch this," he said. He picked up the covers at the end of her bed and uncovered her legs. "Susie," he said in a loud voice, "pick your legs up!" Then, miraculously, both her legs raised up a few inches off the bed. This was almost too much. We all cheered for her. She grinned a mile wide. She wiggled her toes for us. We cheered again. I can't imagine what the other visitors thought about all the hoopla coming out of Susie's room, but we didn't care at the time. No one was telling us to be quiet. This was the first reason to be happy we had had in two days of stress and agony. It was a blessed relief for everyone. Susie had made it through the first 48 hours. Here she was, smiling and moving her legs. We talked to her, laughed and cried with her, watched her smile at us, and Lord knows gave her how many kisses. The thirty minutes was over in an instant. Scott made everyone leave, but let me stay a few extra minutes. By now, Susie was drifting back off.

Alone with her, I called her by name. She moved her head to the sound of my voice, and her eyes barely cracked open. Almost right away, though, they closed again. I would have given anything for her to remain awake with me, if only for a minute, but it was not to be. So I kissed her cheek ever so softly, and whispered into her ear. "Susie, honey, I hope you can hear me. I'm glad you're back. We can lick this thing. You're going to be OK." I felt the tears coming. "I got to go now, sweetie. I love you. But I tell you something. I'll be right down the hall. I'm never going to leave you. I'll always be here. It's you and me for as long as it takes, OK sweetie?" It was all I had. I looked up at Scott. "This is good, right? Her waking up like this?"

He smiled at me. "It's not bad, Rick. It's a big step in the right direction." He let it go at that, and I kissed Susie one more time, told her I loved her, and left her room.

As I walked back to the waiting room, I noticed it was a much different walk than every other time had been. I was a much different Rick. My head seemed a little clearer. Susie had opened her eyes, she had smiled at me and at everyone else, and she had moved her legs. These were such small, little accomplishments that, only three days ago, would have been so insignificant. Yet, here we were, celebrating as if they were the greatest achievements in the history of the world. Because, for Susie, they were. It was almost as if she were a newborn baby again. Look, everyone! She smiled! And look at her move her head to the sound of my voice! It's funny how things can change so dramatically, and so quickly.

I didn't go back to the waiting room right away. I went downstairs to the chapel. I thanked God over and over. And I told Him that I fully intended to keep my promise. Never again would He be left out of my life. Or out of my family's life. I would talk to my kids about Him. I would never let them forget that He was the reason Susie would live. I vowed they would know Him the way I did now.

Everyone welcomed me with hugs and tears. We were suddenly so optimistic. Jenny kept warning that the road was still long, but that this was a major step down that road. We weren't out of the woods yet, either. No one believed that though, at least not right then. We had seen those big, beautiful brown eyes again, and that lovely white smile! It was Susie, not just her body laying there ravaged with pain and suffering. She was alert and knowing. She was going to make it and be just fine!

Some of Susie's family left to go to church, but I wasn't going anywhere. I was suddenly hungry, and I mentioned there was a Wendy's across the street from the hospital. One of my sisters left to get some burgers, and I sat down on a couch, relief giving way to exhaustion. But sleep was impossible. I gathered my kids around me and we just sat there together. No one said anything, but we were all thinking the same thoughts. Mom would get better. For the first time in two days we could be optimistic. I couldn't wait to tell Scotty.

This episode in Susie's long story would prove to be a lesson to me. I would learn the hard way that the road to Susie's recovery would be a series of advances and setbacks. The roller coaster ride was just beginning and, like Susie's heart attack, would prove to be a doozy. For now, though, I had respite from the agony and fear that had refused to leave me alone for the last two days. I felt better. I could smile and even laugh a little. I could look to the future without such an overwhelming sense of dread.

For a while, at least.

For a while.

CHAPTER NINE:

THE DECISION

And that is when I made my decision. It was an easy decision. There was never even an internal debate. I looked over at Scott. "You know," I said, "I won't let her live like that."

He understood.

This is a difficult chapter to start because it was a difficult chapter in my life, and in Susie's life. Looking back now, this was the beginning of the end of life as we knew it.

Does that sound funny? Because, realistically, wasn't Susie's heart attack the beginning of that end? I don't believe it was. When she woke up on Friday morning, and she began smiling at everyone, following voices around the room, and moving her legs, I firmly believe that her brain was near 100%, if not entirely sound. It was Susie looking back at me through those beautiful brown eyes. What followed after Friday morning, then through the weekend and into the next week, accounted for the most difficult ordeal my family and I could ever have imagined.

Word of Susie's awakening spread quickly through both sides of the family. The visitors, who crowded her room in the final two visits of the day, were incredible. There was standing room only. Everyone wanted to see her perform. I was more to blame than anyone, probably. Blink your eyes! Smile! Move your legs! We would ask her to do these things, and she would usually oblige. More cheers and clapping. It was just so good to see her again, knowing that she understood and was able to accommodate our requests. I noticed, however, by the end of the evening Friday, that she really looked exhausted. Even after I was allowed to stay Friday night I couldn't get a response from her. She could open her eyes, but I could tell she wasn't focusing on me. I didn't push it. Get your rest, I told her; we'll visit again tomorrow. Then I left, eventually leaving the hospital for the first time to be with my kids.

There is something about waking up each morning when you have a loved one in ICU. There is the hope for improvement after a long night. It consumes you. You think, OK, 12 hours have passed; she should be a lot better now. You especially think this when you're told that time will be the biggest healer. Every morning you have that renewed feeling of faith. If she was that good yesterday, you think, she ought to be phenomenal today! You can't wait for that first visit. You walk into her room imagining that she will be sitting up, watching TV and ready to get out of bed anytime now. It's crushing when it doesn't happen.

Saturday morning was this way. Susie was awake, and she looked at me, but it was far from how she was the day before. There was no eye blinking or leg movement at all. And I began to notice the total lack of movements in her arms and hands. I longed for her to squeeze my hands. I asked her over and over. It was disappointing when I knew she could hear me, when she could blink and wiggle her toes on command, yet she had not once squeezed my hand. I also missed kissing her on the lips. With the breathing tube, it was impossible. I would kiss her hand, her cheek, her nose and her forehead. But how I missed those lips! It is amazing what you can take for granted when the world goes as planned. I longed to hold her hand and walk with her. What a simple act. We did it all the time. Yet, at this point in time, it was impossible and would not happen again for a long time.

I also missed talking with her. We spent so much time together. We would talk about everything from the kids, our future, the business and how well it was doing, to casinos and when we were going next. She had not uttered a word in four days. I also missed holding her, particularly at night. Rarely would a night go by, even after 21 years of marriage, that she didn't turn over and put her head on my shoulder or chest. I always slept on my back so this was easy for her to do. I missed her saying "Hey Rick!" when she would call on her cell phone, the way she started every conversation with me, every time she would go anywhere in her Excursion. Such a simple thing; now, so important to me. It got to be almost a ritual. I think she called on purpose so I would say, "You just can't drive without using that cell phone, can you?" I could go on and on. I missed everything about our lives together.

So she was awake, but she wasn't. After the 8:30 visit, her father gathered everyone together. "We are going to have some rules about visiting Susie from now on. We're going to have no more than four in her room at one time, and the rest need to wait outside the ICU until someone comes out, then we can switch. I think we wore her out yesterday. She needs her rest." They were good rules. She did need her rest, and I agreed with everything he said. I just hoped he understood that I had to always be one of those four in her room, especially at this early stage in her recovery. Once her nurses began to give me leeway, however, I would usually stay outside her room while everyone else visited. It was far better with just Susie and me alone.

These new rules didn't improve her condition, though. Throughout the day Saturday she seemed to become more and more listless. The smiles were few, and in fact by the end of the night had stopped completely. Her eyes would open but not focus. Her leg movements ceased. Her head would move from side to side but not for any particular purpose. It seemed to be purely restless motion. And she would gag and cough. I knew how much she hated that breathing tube; I got to where I hated it more than she did. I kept a close watch on the settings. By Saturday night the machine was only breathing for her twice a minute, and the oxygen was on the lowest setting before the tube would be pulled. Scott was sure that she could breathe on her own and that the tube would be pulled at least by Sunday afternoon. This was great news. I was sure that by removing this object from her throat she would make great strides toward recovery.

As out of it as she was by Saturday night, I still enjoyed our visit. I was allowed to stay until almost 10:00, a full hour past normal visitation. By now I had gotten to know all of the nurses. They knew how important it was for me to spend as much time with Susie as possible. They gave us our space. I was so grateful for that. I don't know how many rules they broke for me, but I'll never tell.

They would also listen to me. I mean, listen and listen and listen. Without interruption. I told them about Susie and our kids. They would listen to me talk about our business and our plans. They became acutely aware of the special relationship Susie and I had.

I don't know whether or not that by the nurses becoming so close to us, and make no mistake, we were and still are close, it helped with Susie's care. I know how professional the entire staff was at all times with every patient. Still, I can't help but believe that just maybe we gained a slight edge over the odds. If nothing else, perhaps they all prayed a little harder and a little more often. I'll take it. I do feel that, because of our time together, I was given tremendous leeway with extended visitation. I would call 10 or 15 minutes before, you know, just to see how she was, and then ask if I could go ahead and come back. They all knew exactly what I was doing, and nearly every time would say yes. I never saw anyone else visiting the way I did. I don't know if they didn't know, didn't try, or what. I never said anything, though. I was not going to rock the boat.

That time alone with Susie meant the world to me. Besides doing all the cosmetic things with her hair and lips, I would also talk endlessly to her. I would convince her that she was going to make it, that we were not going to work as hard as we used to and that I would always be there for her while she recovered, no matter how long it took. I told her how much the kids missed her, especially Scotty. I never wanted her to feel alone. I told her again and again that, even if I wasn't in the room with her, I was always just down the hall. I didn't know what else to say. I just wanted her to hear me.

So I stayed with her that Saturday night until 10:00, and it was wonderful. Make no mistake; I was worried sick about her condition when I left, but I still felt she would recover, and it was the most time alone I had had with her since her admittance Wednesday afternoon. I stopped by the waiting room before I went home. There were still some people there that were not staying the night. "You've been in there with her the whole time? I thought you had already gone home!" They were envious, and I understood. But they were happy for me as well. I went home to my kids, tired but optimistic.

That would change early Sunday morning. I woke up about 3:30 and stared up at the ceiling. I would do this a lot while Susie was in the hospital. I would lay there, the thoughts going through my head at the rate of about a thousand a minute, until further sleep was impossible. I had the number to the ICU memorized, and reached for the cordless I always kept beside my bed. I dialed the numbers. Vonda was on nights every weekend. I asked for her, and she answered immediately. "This is Vonda."

"Vonda, Rick here. How's our girl doing?" Again, it was morning after a long, restful night. I had no anticipation of any bad news. That was short-lived.

"Rick, it has not been a good night."

I sat up quickly. My heart began racing. The only thing I could imagine was her heart had stopped again. "What's wrong, Vonda?"

"Jan has been in her room with me since 3:00. We can't get her to wake up. We've tried everything. I even had "Grease" playing on a boom box right beside her. I had it up loud, too. She just will not open her eyes. It's been like this since you left last night."

"I'm on my way." I dressed quickly, not bothering to shower. I drove to the hospital on empty, pre-dawn streets. I ran from the parking lot, up the stairs to the second floor and down that long hallway. The doors opened for me immediately.

I hurried into Susie's room, both Jan and Vonda by her side. Susie lay with her eyes closed, resting easy it seemed to me, no movement whatsoever except for her chest rising up and down. I walked around to my side of the bed and next to Jan. She looked like hell. She obviously had had no sleep and I think she was happy to get some relief. I looked at Vonda. "How's she doing?"

"The same, Rick. She won't wake up." She looked at Susie. "SUSIE!" I jumped. I had not expected her to yell her

name that loud. "WAKE UP, HONEY! YOU'RE HUS-
BAND'S HERE!"

Nothing. Her eyelids didn't flinch. I tried. "Hey, sweetie.
It's me." I leaned down to her ear. "Susie, can you hear me?
C'mon, honey, open your eyes for me."

Nothing worked. The only time she would open her eyes
at all was when she gagged or coughed through the breathing
tube. There was no focus whatsoever, only a blank stare. She
was seeing nothing. Someone shined a light in her eyes but
there was very little pupil activity. I began to get a severe
sense of dread.

Jan went home to shower and rest. I stayed with Susie the
rest of that morning and was there when the 8:30 visitors
began filing in. I never left her side. Everyone's mood was
very somber, a stark contrast from just 24 hours ago. Nothing
anyone did would bring her around. Her mom's voice, her
dad's voice and over and over again my voice wouldn't pro-
duce any movement at all. Only that damn breathing tube
would get her to move. I even had a fear that it was the reason she had taken a turn backwards. She so hated that thing
in her throat. I felt that maybe it was her way of not having to
deal with it - just stay asleep and it won't hurt anymore. I
asked her nurses about that theory. They didn't count it out. I
asked them if backing down on the morphine would help her
wake up. They had already thought of that.

Jenny, our family nurse, had other ideas. She felt the anti-
seizure drug Dilantin was the culprit. They had begun administering the drug the day before. We asked Dr. Pulan about
this when she made her morning rounds. Could this be a reason that Susie is suddenly comatose?

"It could be, but I don't think so. I think it has more to do
with her brain swelling."

Then Dr. Pulan began experimenting with Susie's feet.
She took her pen and ran the end of it along the bottom of her
feet. Her toes instantly curled inward. She frowned at Susie's
reaction. "She is posturing. This is bad."

"Doctor," I said, "what is posturing?" I couldn't believe she had said "this is bad" the same way she might have ordered something to eat from a menu. I understand that medical professionals must remain impartial. She had this part of her job down pat. Whatever came to her mind, she would say it. Susie was simply chart number whatever to her.

"Posturing is the brain's way of reacting to stimuli when normal function is gone."

I was in the twilight zone now. I tried to think clearly, ask questions intelligently. "Doc, she's not brain dead is she? I mean, yesterday she was fine. She knew us. Hell, she knew what the casinos were."

"Mr. Jacobs, I warned you about the brain swelling. Her heart attack was when, Wednesday?"

"Yeah, Wednesday afternoon."

"This is Sunday morning. This afternoon will only be the fourth day since the trauma occurred. Her brain is trying to swell but has nowhere to go. At least this is what I suspect is happening. We will know a lot more in the next five to seven days. This should be ample time for the swelling to subside. I don't believe she will remain this way; at least she won't be brain dead. But there is no way of knowing, right now, how much damage has occurred or where the damage will be. We could stay where we are, recover completely or anywhere in between."

I stared at the doctor. Stay the way she is? *Stay the way she is?* I refused to believe that. I didn't know what to ask her. So I mumbled some thanks, and then she left. I sat down on my chair beside her bed, put her hand inside both of mine and then held it against my face. I watched her as she slept. Occasionally she would convulse and gag on the tube. I asked someone - I couldn't tell you who was in the room - if the doctor still planned to remove it later today - and they said they would try to find out. There was a feeding tube in her nose, where she ate and drank. I suddenly realized that no food or water had gone down her throat since her heart attack. How dry her throat must feel! The occasional alarm would go off. The sound of IV boxes automatically whirring in her drugs rhythmically filled the room. How in the hell did she end up like this? This was now Susie's world. This was now my world. My God!

The hardest realization during this difficult time was that it was all just beginning. Only four days had gone by and no way of knowing how many weeks or months of, Lord willing, recovery there would be. This was so tough to accept and understand. It's only been four days? It seemed an eternity. A lot of it had to do with the nearly total lack of sleep. Some of it was the excruciatingly long hours between visits. Still, the reality of just how long a road lie before us was frightening. I began to wonder if I could do it.

I waited. I waited throughout the entire Sunday. Every visitation, I hoped against hope that Susie's neurologist might be wrong. Maybe Susie was just really tired, and this afternoon she would be back the way she was on Friday. She didn't wake up, though, at 12:30, 5:30, or 8:30. I was devastated. It was that roller coaster, that up and down ride, that was making me crazy. I learned to build a wall around myself, an impenetrable wall that protected me from any kind of news, good or bad. No more would I allow myself to get my hopes up, only to be slammed back down, harder than before. It was just too hard. Way too hard.

On the last visit of Sunday evening, Scott was in Susie's room with me. I was too down to talk much. It was about 9:30 and I was ready to leave when I said, "Scott, pretend I'm another nurse. Or I'm a doctor, and we are discussing Susie's condition and recovery. You know, her prognosis. Tell me about her, Scott. Just what exactly are we looking at here?"

He looked at me, unsure at first how to answer. "Are you sure, Rick?"

I nodded. "Scott, I'll go out of my mind quicker not knowing. You've seen this before. Based on your experience, what can I expect?"

He took a deep breath. "I wondered when you would ask. Rick, I've seen hundreds of cases like this. Point blank, she probably won't get much better. She may wake up, she may not. If she does, I doubt she'll ever get out of bed. She probably will never talk again or be able to eat or drink again. Her heart stopped for a long time, Rick. I believe there is a lot of brain damage."

I absorbed it all. "So, more or less a vegetable, if she wakes up?"

He nodded. "That's what I believe will happen, Rick."

"Scott, is there any chance you may be wrong? I mean, could she still get better? Even a lot better?"

He shook his head. "Rick, I have seen miracles, and that's exactly what it would take. It would take a miracle. Prayer is the only chance she has. I told you before that I've seen prayer work when nothing else could. Right now, in my opinion, that's what is left."

So, there it was. Like a punch in the stomach, or rather a cannonball shot from close range, Scott told me the way it was. It was strange to me I didn't cry. You get news like that and you cry, don't you? Susie may not wake up. Even if she does, she won't be Susie, really. She'll lie in a bed for the next 30 years or so, and won't know anything. And that is when I made my decision. I looked over at Scott. "You know," I said, "I won't let her live like that."

He understood. "That's completely your decision, Rick."

"No, not really. It was our decision. We've talked about it before. I wouldn't want her to let me live that way; she wouldn't want to live that way. I just never figured it would ever happen - at least not this soon." I looked down at Susie as I talked, not believing I was talking about her. And for the first time, I began to look at her as if Susie, my Susie, was no longer lying there. Here was a body, a ravaged body that had been through hell, carrying the only woman I ever truly loved. But if her brain was gone, I realized, so was Susie. I looked at the clock; it was 10:00. I needed to be home. More than ever,

I needed to hug my kids. "I got to go, Scott."

Before I left though, I went over to him, and I held out my hand. He took my hand, then pulled me towards him put his arms around me. It was comforting. I had made such a huge decision, a life altering decision; an irreversible decision and he had accepted it completely. I felt close to him because he had been so honest with me, and told me what I had to know. Or maybe it was a combination of all that we had been through together. Whatever it was, a bond formed between us that remains strong to this day and will likely last forever. I'll never forget that part of my life for as long as I live. It's not a conversation you have every day. It's not one I expected to have about Susie.

I had made my decision and I was OK with it. I still had time. I still had hope. Susie hadn't left us yet. She wasn't past the point of no return. I would still pray for her. I would still cry for her at night. I would remain at her side every day for as long as there was still breath in her body. But, when the time came, if it came, I had made my decision.

It was a decision that would not come without consequences, however. There were those who could not, or would not, understand that I could make such a decision. That, because I loved this woman so much, I could do this *for* her, not *to* her. And, had the roles been reversed, she would do the same for me.

Neither of us would have had it any other way.

CHAPTER TEN:

THE MEETING

He then put his Barney pillow on my chest and snuggled next to me. I put my arm around him and we both fell asleep. He would sleep on his mom's side of the bed every night after that until she came home.

I guess it was the next best thing to her being there.

Monday and Tuesday, September 10th and 11th, were probably the two most difficult days of my life. Susie's nurses allowed me all the time with her I wanted, and I was by her side eight to ten hours a day, looking for something, anything, that would give me cause for hope.

There was nothing.

The only time I left her room was during normal visitation, so others could have the whole time. They didn't know what I knew at that time. They were waiting for her full recovery and never thought otherwise. I hadn't given up all hope. I felt like I had to look at the situation realistically. I owed this to myself, my kids and even to Susie. I would accept whatever God had decided. I hoped He would bring her back, but either way I would be prepared.

The hours I had her to myself were difficult. She simply wasn't there. Nothing I said or did produced any reaction at all. I begged her to wake up. I pleaded with her, "Susie, can you hear me? If you can hear me, sweetie, follow the sound of my voice. If you're in a dark room, and you can't find your way out, listen to me. Follow the sound of my voice. I know you're scared; so am I. But we can fight this, Susie, we can beat this thing. You have four kids who need you, babe; they need their mom. I can't do this by myself. We've made plans that you got to be here for. We have a 25th wedding anniversary cruise to take, remember? To Hawaii? Thanksgiving and Christmas is just around the corner - what would the holidays be like without you? Come on, Susie! Fight it, sweetie! Don't give up! Don't give up!"

I even sang to her. There's a great country song called "And We Danced" that was one of her favorites. We used to love to slow dance together. I would say to her, "We've got a lot of dances left, right? I'll put my arms around you, and you'll put your head on my shoulder, just like we used to, OK?" And then I would put my arms around her, put my head on her shoulder and sing the words to the song, very softly, right into her ear. Countless times I sang this song to her.

But nothing worked. As time went on I became more and more discouraged. I knew I was neglecting my kids during this period, but I needed to be with Susie more than anything in the world. And I felt she needed me right then more than the kids did as well. Also, I wanted to be there in case anything, one way or the other, happened. When she opened her eyes, I would be there. If she opened her eyes.

Scott gave me a pager late Tuesday night as I was leaving. He showed me how to work it, said it had a 25-mile range and was hooked through the computer in the ICU. He knew how exhausted I was, and he hoped it would help me sleep. "Anything happens, Rick, I mean anything, and I will page you, OK?"

I nodded, hooked it to my belt, and left. It was nearly 11:00 before I closed my eyes. I fell asleep immediately.

It was 3:40 Wednesday morning when the pager went off, the electronic tones filling my room, and at first I had no earthly idea what they were. I turned my lamp on and confusion finally gave way to the realization, *It's the pager!* I picked it up, my hands shaking so badly I couldn't press the right buttons. *Come on, damn it! How do you get to the text?* Finally, my mind cleared a little, and I was able to read Scott's message:

Rick, Susie is awake! You can come see her now!

I have no recollection whatsoever of dressing, driving to the hospital or running from the car to the ICU. When I got to her room, I was shocked to see her breathing tube had been removed! They had taken it out the night before. I knew that it was imminent; she had realistically been breathing on her own for three days at least, but they were concerned about her comatose condition. I was thrilled to see it gone. Scott, of course, was in the room. He said, "Susie? Rick's here." Her eyes fluttered, then opened a little. She seemed to look at me, but I didn't see any recognition. She stretched a little, and I was happy to see her legs move ever so slightly, but her arms remained motionless, as if made of concrete.

I took her hand, then bent over and kissed her on the lips. On the lips! What a thrill that was, to finally, once again, kiss Susie on the lips! "Susie? Can you hear me, sweetie? It's your husband." Again, her eyelids moved a little, trying to open. It was as if they were glued shut, and it was a supreme effort to get them open. She finally looked at me. There was no smile; there was no expression at all. Then she looked as if she was going to gag, and the coughing started. The amount of phlegm in her throat after a week of that breathing tube was phenomenal. Scott was immediately by her side, suction tube in hand. It was like a dentist's suction, only bigger in diameter. Scott waited until Susie opened her mouth to cough and then inserted the suction tube deep. He explored until he was rewarded with tons of the stuff being sucked out of her throat. Susie would move her head from side to side, her facial expressions becoming more and more agitated. She despised that tube. She would hear the sucking noise it made from a mile away, and would turn her head away even before she saw the mouthpiece. She would clamp her teeth together tight and sometimes growl as if warning to keep the thing away. It would be a three week long battle. She would fight anything going into her mouth for a long time. I figured it reminded her of that horrible breathing tube. Scott told me that, far and away, patients remembered the breathing tube as the worst part of the ICU experience, if they remembered anything.

I stayed with her until 6 a.m. She remained awake much of the time, coughing constantly, fighting Scott and the suction tube. She would react to the sound of my voice by turning her head towards me, but there were no smiles. There was also no response whatsoever to any commands from either Scott or myself. She would not raise her legs, wiggle her toes or even blink her eyes. The expression "the lights are on but nobody's home" totally applied here. I longed for some sort of recognition, some inkling of awareness from her, but I found nothing. I was a little discouraged when I left her room, but I reminded myself it was better than what we had had for more than two days. At least she was awake - maybe awareness would come a little bit at a time.

I often compared my situation using a football analogy, and Susie and I were on the enemy's one-inch line. Going backwards was not an option. I would hand the ball to Susie, and she would gain six inches at a time. Almost imperceptible, yet they were gains. We had a hell of a long way to go. It would seem impossible to fathom at times, yet I had to remain focused on the goal, not the distance. Sometimes it was difficult to remember this.

I went to the ICU waiting room and woke Jan. When she was able to finally focus on me, she panicked.

I calmed her. "It's OK, Jan. Scott paged me. Susie's awake." She was up instantly and began to put her shoes on. "I'm going back home and take a shower. I'll get Scotty on the bus and then come relieve you. I'll call the rest of the family from the house and give them the news. You just go see Susie and not worry about calling anyone." She said thank you, hugged me, and was out the door to see her sister.

I drove back to the house and woke up the kids. I gave them the news about Susie and, of course, they were happy. I cautioned them that, at least when I had left the hospital, she still did not seem aware of anything. But who knows what may happen between now and the end of the day. They begged me to let them stay home and go to the hospital, but I said no. Reluctantly, they went to get ready.

I must have made ten or fifteen phone calls. I found myself becoming more and more excited with every person I told the news to. I would regret that later. I had told myself not to get my hopes up every time Susie seemed to improve. It got to be too devastating when she would have a setback. I wanted to be cautiously optimistic. I would build that wall around me, telling myself to peek over the top edge when good news would come, but then quickly retreat down inside the safe confines of that wall to keep from being shot down all at once. But I would allow myself, sometimes, to tear down the wall completely and revel in any sort of good news with everyone else. The roller coaster.

I realized on the way back to the hospital that morning that this was the one-week anniversary of Susie's heart attack. Happy anniversary, huh? What a week it had been! It seemed like a year, although I had aged twenty. I wondered what would happen next.

When I had gotten back to the hospital I found that every person I called was there for the first visit of the morning. I couldn't blame them - it had been so long since anyone had seen Susie's eyes. I found Jan and took her to the side. "Was she awake for you?" Please, give me good news.

"She never smiled or anything, Rick. I don't even think she knew me. Was she like that for you earlier?" I told her she was. Still, we remained optimistic. There was always one advantage that we held over every other patient in the ICU - time. We had time. Susie was only 39. If it took 10 years for her to recover completely, then so be it. She would only be 49. The length of her recovery never scared me - only the lack of her recovery did.

They let me in her room early, and I went to her full of anticipation. There was no change, however. She would open her eyes for a little while, and then drift off to sleep again. She wouldn't blink, wouldn't smile. I put Vaseline on her lips - they were horribly chapped and sore - and combed her hair for the visitors she was about to have. I talked to her, trying to make her understand who came to see her: her mom and dad, our daughter Lisa, all her brothers and sisters. But there was no reaction at all. And that didn't change when everyone began to arrive. Susie did open her eyes, and she would follow the sound of voices, but her expression never changed, emotionless and empty. Everyone was thrilled to see that the breathing tube was gone, but at the same time agonized over the obvious suffering Susie was going through trying to clear her throat and lungs. As terrible as the suction tube was for her, it was important that fluids remained out of her lungs. Pneumonia was a very real threat.

I stayed by Susie's side all day Wednesday, leaving only to briefly eat something or to make phone calls. I talked to her constantly - it was amazing how easily the words came. I never ran out of things to say. I also sang to her. With each passing hour, however, I found myself losing hope. When doctors or nurses came in I would ask questions. The answers were always the same.

By late Wednesday night, I was devastated. When I looked at Susie, I saw a body going through the motions of basic, instinctive survival. She could breathe, her bodily functions remained intact, her heart had stabilized and was beating normally. She couldn't move, however, or talk, or smile, or recognize her loved ones. She couldn't eat or drink, or do anything that made her Susie. The woman I loved, the mother of my children, the very person who made my life worth living, was, at that point in time, gone. I sat by her bedside, held her hand, and watched her. Her eyes opened now and then, but I had long given up trying to get any reaction from her. Her breathing was loud, always through her mouth and would pass through the ever-present fluid in the back of her throat. She would put off coughing until she absolutely had no choice, because she knew the dreaded suction tube would follow. She reached the point where, when you could finally pry her teeth apart to get it in her mouth, she would clamp down on the plastic tube to keep you from moving it around. I swear I think she was trying to bite it in two. I felt, at that time, it was all instinctive, though. Hope gave way to resignation. Susie was gone. She wasn't coming back. I had to prepare myself for the inevitability. I hadn't yet completely given up, but I was close.

I asked God that night not to prolong it, if this was His will. I didn't want to lose her, but it was far worse watching her suffer this way. This once beautiful, vibrant, incredibly smart and independent woman had been reduced to this animal-like condition. One who would bare her teeth and growl in anger at the suction tube. It was too much to witness, too cruel to comprehend.

When I left the hospital Wednesday night it was late. I drove home in a complete daze, my subconscious taking over the motions of stopping at lights and stop signs. I was trying to imagine a world without her. I had lived with this woman for nearly 21 years. She was always going to be a part of my life, or at least until we were very old. I got home and walked into the kitchen. It was very quiet; the kids were apparently asleep. I stood in the kitchen, frozen in time, thoughts of Susie dominating everything else. I don't know how long I stood there, but I was brought back when I heard, "How's Mommy, Daddy?" It was Scotty, standing at the entrance to the kitchen. His thumb was in his mouth, the ever-present Barney pillow tucked under his arm, his eyes just barely open. I went to him and put my arms around him. He hugged me back and it was incredibly comforting. I felt the tears coming, and it took everything I had in me to maintain control.

"She's still really sick, Scotty. I know she misses you a lot."

"I miss her too, Daddy. How come I can't see her?" I wondered when he would ask this.

"I'll take you to see her real soon, big guy, I promise. Right now you need to go back to bed."

"Can I sleep in your bed tonight?" What could I do? I picked him up, and he lay his head on my shoulder as we walked into my bedroom. I laid him down on Susie's side of the bed and covered him up. The thumb went back into his mouth and his eyes were closed instantly. I watched him for a while. I rubbed his back for a minute and then kissed him. When I got into bed and turned out the lamp, he stirred. He then put his Barney pillow on my chest and snuggled next to me. I put my arm around him, and we both fell asleep. He would sleep on his mom's side of the bed every night after that until she came home. I guess it was the next best thing to her being there.

Thursday morning began normally enough. I got Scotty up, dressed and fed, and then sat with him at his bus stop, as I had done every morning since Susie's illness, until his bus picked him up. I really enjoyed this part of my day. We would get there ten or fifteen minutes early and just talk about anything and everything. The subject of Susie rarely came up. Mostly we talked about school and the things he did at Aunt Beth's house. Beth was Susie's best friend, and she had been picking up Scotty every afternoon after school. She also had four kids, and her two older boys took Scotty under their wings and had a ball with him. Beth made sure his homework got done, fed him and brought him home every night. She was also a good listener for me. There was more than one night where we talked outside in my driveway. We reminisced about Susie and the great times we had together. We laughed and cried together, and I always felt better afterwards.

When I got to the hospital, I went straight to Susie. I didn't stop at the waiting room. I was so hoping that the night had been good for her, that she had gotten lots of rest and would be improved. Her nurse was somber. Her condition was the same, she told me, and she was so sorry. I went to my usual spot and held Susie's hand. I began talking to her, telling her about Scotty the night before and that he wanted to see her. You'll have to get better, I told her, before I bring Scotty for a visit. I didn't want him to see her unless I knew she would recognize him. I prayed silently it would happen.

Throughout the long morning I remained vigilantly by her side. I felt the hours slipping by, my time with her growing shorter and shorter. She showed no signs of improvement at all, no recognition of anything or anyone whatsoever. I could feel all hope disappearing, despair growing and the inevitable becoming more and more obvious. Just before the 12:30 visitation, I called the waiting room and asked for my daughter. Lisa came to the phone. "Sweetie, come over to the room, but just you."

Lisa stood at the door, afraid to come in. There was the slightest trace of tears in her eyes. I'm sure she knew what was coming. I walked over to her and put my arms around her. I hugged her for a long time. I looked over at her mom and said, "Susie, Lisa's here." Susie moved her head to the sound, but there was nothing there. She moved her head the other way and then closed her eyes. She coughed a little, but not enough to warrant suctioning her throat. At that moment, Dr. Kennedy, her pulmonary doctor, came in.

"Dr. Kennedy, I'm glad you're here. I want you to tell us straight. How much better will Susie get?" I felt Lisa's arms tighten up just a little on me, and I hugged her a little harder as well. Dr. Kennedy looked at me as if to ask "Are you sure?" and I said, "It's OK." She put her clipboard down, and began.

"I don't think she will. I feel there is too much damage neurologically. I was surprised she even woke up." Lisa began to cry, and she buried her face in my chest.

"Doc," I said, "how will she eat? Will that tube stay in her nose for the rest of her life?"

She shook her head. "No, Rick, the nose tube can only stay in for three weeks. Then we'll have to put in a stomach tube. She can be fed indefinitely through that."

I took a deep breath. "Then what? A nursing home?" Dr. Kennedy nodded. "So," I said, "she'll exist the way she is now for the next 30 or 40 years, barring some miracle?" Dr. Kennedy nodded once again. I then asked the question I had been dreading, the question I had to know. "Do I have to allow the feeding tube?"

"No Rick, you don't."

It's funny, but, again, I wasn't crying here. I felt little emotion, and I felt a little guilty. I don't know if I was all cried out, or if I was just relieved to be finally talking about it. It had been a terrible week, full of ups and downs. It was as if I was in a batter's box and God was pitching. He would throw me an inside fast ball and knock me down. Each time He did, it became harder to stand back up. I would look at God on the pitcher's mound, and He'd be smiling at me, throwing the ball up and down, catching it in His hand. He'd look at me and say, "Whatcha gonna do, Rick? You gonna stay down this time? You got anything left?" I'd look into the stands, and I would see my kids. They were standing, watching, waiting to see what I would do, and pleading with their eyes for me to be strong for them. So I would somehow get back up, dust myself off, and wait for the next pitch. So maybe there was relief, that at last I knew where we were going. That I now had some control over Susie's care and future. I don't really know what I was feeling, exactly. This was all new to me. This was not something you learned in school. I asked the doctor, "What then?"

She said, "We'll put her on a morphine drip. She'll go to sleep and not wake up. She'll be completely pain free."

The voice behind me was choked with emotion. "I would hope, Rick, that before you decide something like this you'll get with her family first." It was Susie's father. It was visitation time and he had come back to see her.

I don't know how much he heard, but apparently it had been enough to understand what I had decided to do. I was still holding Lisa, and didn't turn around to face him. I just said, "Mac, she's not going to get any better."

"How do you know that?"

"Dr. Kennedy," I said, "would you explain to him what you told us earlier?" And she did. He listened without comment. As she got to the end, Susie's mother walked in. She saw me holding Lisa; she noticed her husband was emotional, and it scared her.

"What's going on here? What's the matter?"

Mac spoke up. "Susie's pretty sick, Ma."

She began to get scared. "I know she is, but she'll get better. She's going to get better."

"Mom," I said, "she's not going to get better! Dr. Kennedy, tell her!"

But she wouldn't listen. "I'm not going to hear this. I am not going to hear this." She walked out, and Mac went with her. The room was suddenly quiet; Lisa's gentle sobs were the only sound at all. Dr. Kennedy walked around us, understanding we needed to be alone, and left the room. After a minute I spoke to my daughter, "You know, kid, we're lucky, me and you. We had her longer than anybody. Poor Scotty, he'll never know her the way we did." Lisa looked at me through red, tear- filled eyes. "Lisa, can you understand how I can't allow her to live this way? We've talked about it, neither of us wants this. This is not living."

Lisa, God bless her, was wonderful. "Dad, I know. I don't want her living like this, either. I want to remember Mom the way she was, not like now."

I hugged her all over again. Thank God for this little girl. She was one of the best things Susie and I ever did. I told her, "Lisa, we still have two weeks before I have to decide anything. She could get better. We have to hope for just that. We have to ask God to get her better. We have two weeks." Lisa nodded, and then she had to go. I went to Susie and held her hand. "What are you going to do, Babe? God, please tell me, what are you going to do?" I put my head on her chest and wept.

Another voice in the door. "Rick! Don't do it! It's against the law!" It was my brother, Mitch. I looked at him, puzzled. "What are you talking about?"

"Don't pull the feeding tube! You'll go to jail!"

I was stunned. "Pull the feeding tube? I'm not pulling the feeding tube. Good God, who told you that?"

He came over to me, and pulled me away from Susie, as if afraid this is what I would do. "Mac's talking about it. He said he heard you talking to the doctor about pulling the tube."

"Mitch," I said, trying to free myself from his grip, "I'm not going to do it now! It was never right now! I've got two weeks to see if she gets better or not. Let go of me!"

He did. "Rick, she could still get better."

"I know that, Mitch. I haven't given up. But if she stays like this, I won't allow her to live like a vegetable in some nursing home for the rest of her life. It wouldn't be fair to her or us!" He looked at her, and he was calmer. Then Mac was back in her room.

"Mitch, can I talk to Rick?" Mitch left. "Rick," he said, "you've never been very good at listening to anyone, but you're going to listen to me. First of all, what you want to do is illegal. By law, you can't touch my daughter. Second, we're going to have a family meeting in half an hour in the chapel downstairs. Nobody but our immediate family will be allowed. None of the Jacobs. And we're gonna talk about this. Let me tell you something, Rick, you don't know what you've got here. Us men are lucky, we come home from work, sit in our recliner, and watch TV. Susie here, she had to work and then come home and cook, take care of the kids and everything else. You never appreciated that..."

I stopped him. What the hell was he talking about? "Wait a minute, Mac, don't you think for one minute that I don't know how special this girl is. I am not blind, for Christ sake."

He wasn't deterred. "Half an hour, Rick." Then he was gone.

I stayed with Susie for that half hour. I took care of her. I combed her hair, suctioned her throat and talked to her. She looked at me through unrecognizing eyes, moved her head from side to side and, as always, breathed noisily through the ever present fluid. It was agonizing for me. How did she feel right now, I wondered? What was going through what was left of her mind? Was her body more or less on autopilot? How I wished I could trade places with her. I deserved this a lot more than she did.

A nurse informed me that Susie would be moving to the acute care floor later that day, as soon as a bed became available. She was living completely on her own now. Other than the feeding tube through her nose, all other support had been removed. She was ready to move up. I was told there would be no more restrictions on visitation, and I could now spend the night in her room if I wanted to. I was glad - I needed some good news.

They sent Lisa to come and get me for the meeting. I didn't know what to expect. I guessed that they would try to talk me out of my decision. Lisa and I took the stairs down and went to the chapel. We didn't talk. With my arm around her, we walked in silence. We found ourselves at the door and went inside. Everyone was already there. Susie's mom and dad, her three brothers, Jan and Jenny were all seated around the room. I avoided eye contact, and Lisa and I found two chairs and sat down. Mac began. "First of all, I want this to be civil. There will be no voices raised in anger. We can talk about this and decide what we're going to do about Susie quietly. I want Jenny to start."

Jenny was ready. "First of all, I want everyone to understand that this will be a long, long road. She could be in rehabilitation for months or even years. She'll move from the room she's in now to a level two care unit, and from there either to a skilled nursing center or straight to aggressive rehabilitation. I hope she can go straight to rehab."

I couldn't believe it. They had everything planned out. They had already made all the decisions without me. I stayed quiet. Jenny tried to continue. "What we have to do right now is stay patient. This won't happen overnight…."

Susie's brother Jimmy interrupted her. "Forget all that! I want to know who's giving up here? Who's throwing in the towel?" He had stood up and was looking directly at me. Mac's instructions of low voice levels were forgotten. Mac tried to keep order. "Sit down, Jimmy, and let Jenny finish."

I was ready, though. They were deciding what would happen to Susie without me, and I resented it. I stood up. "No, Mac, I know who he's talking to. I'll answer him." I walked around the room, this time making eye contact with everyone there. "You know, you guys are lucky. Every night you go home to someone. Every night you have someone to talk to, someone to hold, someone to help you get through all of this. I don't. I don't because the woman I love more than life itself is lying in a room upstairs barely alive. If you guys think this has been easy, you better think again."

Susie's mom spoke up. "Rick, no one here doubts you love Susie..."

I wasn't through, and I didn't interrupt them when they were talking. "Let me finish..." But it wasn't going to happen. It was Jimmy again. He stood up, furious. "Why are you giving up, Rick? What happened to until death do us part? What happened to for better or for worse?" He had that look. What I said didn't matter. He had already made up his mind about me.

I looked at him, disbelieving. I could not comprehend what he was insinuating. I shook my head and said, "I don't have to listen to this." I went to the door. Someone was trying to tell me not to leave, but there was no way I was going to stay. I knew where this was going. The meeting was over. I walked out and didn't look back. I went straight to Susie. I needed to be with her. Only when I had her hand in mine did I remember that I had left Lisa in the chapel. I wondered how that was going. In a way, I was glad she stayed. I could find out what was said after I left.

I looked at Susie, rubbed her hand and arm, and said, "Well, sweetie, they hate me now. They don't understand. This is just what we needed, isn't it? What do we do now, kid? What do we do now?" Of course, she didn't answer. She didn't do anything. She was blissfully unaware of what had just transpired. I was torn up inside. They had no idea what I was thinking, and I wasn't able to tell them - Jimmy had taken care of that. How could I get them to understand? Then I had an idea. A hospital Chaplin had been by to see Susie several times during her hospital stay. I found the card that he had left. I called the number, and to my great relief he answered the phone. "Chaplin, this is Rick Jacobs. Do you remember me?"

"Of course, Rick. What can I do for you?" His voice was

blessedly soothing; welcome after the harsh words I had heard downstairs.

"Are you busy, sir? Can I come see you?"

"Sure, Rick. Are you on your way?"

"I'll be there in ten minutes." I hung up, and then called the waiting room and asked Jan to meet me outside the ICU. She was soon there and I asked her to go with me to see the Chaplin. She agreed.

The Chaplin's office was only a few doors down from the ICU - literally just around the corner. Neither of us said anything while we walked. I don't know whether or not she had any idea of what I had planned. Maybe she hoped I would be talked out of what I had decided. Maybe she believed her dad - that I could not prevent the stomach tube by law. They were wrong there. It was my choice and my choice alone. I had talked to enough people over the last two days to know where I stood on that issue. That wasn't my intent anyway. My purpose here was to try and explain what I was thinking to Susie's family. The only way that could happen was to hear me out without interruption. The Chaplin's office would provide that opportunity. I knocked on his door. We heard a voice inside invite us in.

His office was small, cozy and bright. There were bookshelves loaded with books; the only other furniture was his desk and two chairs. I shook hands with him and introduced him to Jan. "How can I help you, Rick?" he asked, and offered us the two chairs. I tried to gather my thoughts, and then I stood back up.

"Chaplin, I have some issues. I want to discuss them with you, and I wanted Jan to hear them as well." He nodded, leaning back in his chair, and waited. "Let me give you some background first. Susie and I have been married for almost 21 years. No one, and I mean no one, could love each other any more than we do. We have such a special relationship. If any two people love each other half as much as we do, they are fortunate."

I began walking around. My voice would crack from time to time from emotion, but I managed to keep going. "I'm faced with a situation right now. I have to make a decision. Do I let her live as a vegetable, or allow her to go to heaven, the only place she could be happy? I mean, the doctors want to drill a hole in her stomach and that's how she'll eat for the next 30 or 40 years. That's nice, isn't it? Dinnertime, Susie! Let's have your tube. Hey, wasn't that good?" My voice was heavy with sarcasm here. I described a scene that was hideous to me. It would never happen. "Then, Chaplin, then I take Scotty to visit her. I'll say, here's your mom, Scotty. No, she can't talk to you. She can't see you and she'll never be able to even hold you, but here's your mom. Nice, huh? Come on, Chaplin, I need some answers here. I mean, I'm getting pressure from people who are content to let her live this way. They are willing to wait for God's hand to come out of the sky in, let's say, fifteen, twenty years, and perform a miracle on her. Rise up! You're healed!" Jan was crying, the Chaplin was expressionless. I kept going. "But you know what scares me more than anything, Chaplin? What if she *knows*? People say to me, no way Rick, she doesn't know a thing. But they can't go inside her head. What if, every once in a while, she becomes aware of her... her existence, and she knows what kind of hell on earth she's been condemned to? How horrible would that be? I don't want to take that chance, Chaplin. Would you?"

I waited. He chose his words carefully. "Rick, I honestly don't know what I would do in your situation. I'm glad I don't have to make the decision."

"Oh, *great* answer, Chaplin. Come on! You're the *Chaplin*! You're supposed to give me guidance here! Tell me, what would Jesus do?"

He shook his head. "I don't know, Rick. I just don't know."

"Chaplin, I don't think Jesus would want her to live that way. The only way Susie can watch her kids grow up, the only way she can be truly happy is to be with God in heaven. The only way I'll ever be able to talk to her again is if she's with God. If she's this way in some nursing home from now on, my family and I will never have any closure. That is not Susie in that room over there, at least not if she stays the way she is now. I won't allow her to simply exist. We've talked about it over the years. I'll not allow the stomach tube. I love her too much. It's what she would want. If she could come back to me for just a few seconds, she would say to me, *Rick, don't let them. Let me go*! Can you understand that, Chaplin?" I looked at Jan. "Jan, do you see where I'm coming from now?"

Jan had a Kleenex out and was wiping her eyes. She looked at me, and cried, "Rick, I see your point. I just think it's too soon. Just don't do it now."

I shook my head in disbelief. "Jan! It was never now! We have two weeks before we have to make any decision. We have two weeks to see if she'll get better or not. That's when I have to decide." She stared at me but never said a word.

We left his office. I went to be with Susie; Jan went back to the waiting room. I don't know if she said anything to her family or not. I tried talking to Jimmy during the next visitation. He threw his hands up.

"Rick, I just don't want to talk about it right now!"

I went up to her mom and said, "Mom, I've never told you this before, but I love you dearly. I need you right now."

She just looked at me, then said, "Rick, if you don't want to take care of her, she can stay with me. I'll take care of her, and I don't care if it takes 40 years." And then she walked away.

So there it was. I didn't care. The only thing I cared about was laying in a room in the ICU. We had two weeks to get better. Two excruciatingly long weeks.

Sometime later that afternoon, Susie's neurologist, Dr. Pulan, made her rounds. I saw her from inside Susie's room and I went outside to see her. I asked her if she had a minute to talk. She actually could right then and there. So, outside

Susie's room in the ICU, I asked her what I had asked every-one else.

"Dr. Pulan, you're her neurologist. What are Susie's chances of recovery?"

"It's too early to tell, Mr. Jacobs. The brain is still trying to recover from the trauma. The swelling is still receding. It's only been eight days." Ever so clinical.

I had to know. "Doc, I know all that. But I want you to tell me straight. Based on your past experiences, how much hope should I have that she'll get any better?"

She wouldn't budge. "I can't say right now. I've seen cases that were worse off than her and they made a full recovery. You can't rule out miracles."

"Doc, I'm not talking about miracles! I'm talking about my wife. I can't plan any kind of future for my family and me with you telling me to hope for a miracle! I want some answers. Give me something I can make sound decisions with."

"You know, Mr. Jacobs, you can't take the incident back."

I was stunned. "I what? I can't take the incident back? You *think*, Doc?" Everyone within earshot stopped what they were doing and looked at us. I was livid. "Oh, I can't take it back. Well, thank you for that piece of news. I thought I could maybe just go back in time and start over. What kind of bull-shit piece of medical advice was that? Jesus, Doc, you went to school to learn that?" I embarrassed her, and I knew it. I didn't care. That was a terrible thing to say. She stared at me until I was through.

"Mr. Jacobs, I cannot tell you if she'll recover or how much recovery there will be. We have to wait and see when the swelling is gone. Then you'll know." She left, the conversa-tion over. I went outside then, to find a place to be alone. I found a place at the front of the hospital where I could sit and think. It must have been senior's couples day. I saw fifteen or twenty couples walk by me, all of them 60 or older, and most of them walking hand in hand or arm in arm.

97

I was so jealous! This is what Susie and I were supposed to be doing in twenty years or so. Enjoying each other in our twilight years. Remembering the past, keeping our grandchildren overnight and traveling together. Why were we being cheated out of all this? This was so unfair. I wondered if I would ever understand it.

One of the priests from our church, Father Joel, was in the room when I returned to the ICU. He was seated in my chair when I walked in. I looked at him for a moment. "Who called you?"

He shook his head. "No one, Rick, just a social call."

I didn't believe him. "I'll bet. Well, what did they tell you? That I plan to let her die? That I woke up this morning and said, I know! I'll just get rid of her! Yeah! That'll be the easiest thing to do! Does that sum it up?" I was ready to explode, and he knew it. He came over to me and put his arms around me.

"Rick, why don't you start at the beginning?" And I did. I told him everything. The meeting in the chapel, the one with Jan and the Chaplin - even the one with Dr. Pulan. I poured my heart out. This wonderful man never interrupted, never interjected and not once passed judgment. When I was through, I looked at him, and said, "So tell me, Father. What does the church think of my decision?"

Father Joel then went to Susie, and for several minutes tried to get some sort of response from her. He tried everything. I prayed for a miracle, but it didn't happen. He finally gave up. He touched her forehead, said a prayer for her, and then looked at me. "Rick," he said sadly, "if this is how she remains, I will support your decision." Never have I been so relieved to hear anything in my life. I thanked him. He asked me how I was holding up.

"You know what keeps me going, Father? The fact that I have no regrets whatsoever. I am not in anguish over something I said to her, or should have said, or didn't say. I'm not thinking, Oh Susie, why did I do this to you? about anything.

If I was able to do it all over, I wouldn't change anything. And neither would she, Father. If she could wake up for a second, she would smile at me and say, Hey, Rick. I had a ball! I never laid a hand on her in anger. I was never unfaithful."

"Sounds like she was a lucky woman, Rick."

"Father, I'm not looking for any awards for being a great husband. Reward people for not robbing a bank, you know? With her, it was easy. I'm the lucky one." He didn't say anything else. He laid a hand on my shoulder, asked God to bless me, then left the room. I wondered if he went to the waiting room to tell Susie's family of his support for me. That will be interesting, I thought.

Susie had still not been transferred when I was ready to leave to go home late Thursday night. Scott told me that it would still be that night, just later on. I left a long note on the office door of the head nurse, thanking all the nurses and staff for everything they had done for Susie. It was with a little sadness that I realized I would not be returning to this unit after tonight, at least not to see Susie. I was drained, physically and emotionally. I had told Scott about the meeting with her family and the Chaplin, and with Father Joel, and that my resolve was still as strong as ever. "Why can't they see Scott, that it's because I love her so much I can do this?" He shook his head. It made me sad, and he knew it.

I told him good-bye, and once again he hugged me. Then he told me something I'll never forget. He said, "Rick, I've been doing this for seven years, and you have more courage than anyone I've ever known."

That stopped me cold. I didn't know what to say. He cannot imagine what that meant to me. All I could manage, through tears, was, "Thanks, Scott." I went over to Susie one last time in the ICU, kissed her on the lips, and whispered, "Good-night, sweetie. Get better for me, OK? I'll see you tomorrow in a different room. Hang in there, kid. I love you." I walked out of that room for the last time. I hugged every nurse I saw on the way out. It was very emotional.

Then one of the other nurses said to me, "Rick, you've got more courage than anyone I've ever known." I told her she was the second person that said that to me that night. Maybe it was true after all. I never thought I had been courageous. I just did what I felt I had to do.

Our time in the Cardiovascular Intensive Care Unit had come to an end. It was eight days that Susie cannot remember, but I will never forget. As I walked down that long hallway for the last time, I felt phenomenally weary, as if all of it caught up with me at once. I don't remember if I slept well that night or not; I don't remember anything about the rest of the night. After the day I had, whatever else happened paled in comparison.

But what was to come - that would be a different story altogether.

CHAPTER ELEVEN:

THE REAWAKENING

I walked forward, and when I looked at Susie, her eyes were open, and she looked directly at me and smiled!

Squeals of delight and cheers all around.

S he was out of Intensive Care.

I was glad. Susie was, for the most part, unhooked from all of the scary machines that surrounded her in the ICU. She still had a catheter; her IV ports remained, and the nasal feeding tube, of course, was still there, but the rest were gone. Her color was good - really good considering what she had been through for the past eight days of her life. If we could have put a little makeup on her face, she would've looked nearly normal. She was beautiful. It was hard to imagine how terribly sick she remained.

Susie, because of her heart attack, touched other lives in so many ways. I noticed that both sides of our families seemed to appreciate spouses more than they used to. Hand-holding walking to and from places, more endearments being said, kisses exchanged more often, and lots of physicals were being scheduled. Superhuman efforts were made without hesitation that made it easier for me to stay with Susie. My kids were always taken care of, our business was opened and operated every day. Suddenly, priorities changed. Time, once an afterthought because we had so much of it left, was no longer taken for granted by anyone connected with us.

I thought about all of these things as I drove to the hospital Friday morning, nine days after her heart attack. I wondered what the next two weeks would bring. If these past nine days were any indication, the next two weeks would be an eternity. Time had passed so quickly before Susie's heart attack. It was strange to note how agonizingly slow the days seemed now.

Susie had still been asleep when I called the hospital from home. She was on the fourth floor now, in room 442. As we had been told by the nurses in the ICU, there were no restrictions whatsoever on visitation. Even Scotty was now allowed to see his mom. Also, there would be a cot in her room for us to sleep on at night. We never had to leave her alone again. I was thrilled.

I took the elevator to the fourth floor. It was weird not getting out on the second floor to the Intensive Care Unit and waiting room. As I neared her room, I noticed that this floor resembled the floors where Susie stayed when all of our children were born. How I wished this was the reason we were here today. What a miracle birth was. I was in all four delivery rooms and witnessed the birth of all our children. How unlucky fathers were in the days where they waited outside these rooms. To see a life begin - to be there at the instant your child takes his first breath, well, it's a thrill that I cannot even hope to ever have the skills to describe.

But, that was not why we were here. We were here because, instead of life beginning, we were praying that life would not be ending. I had starting adding a postscript to my prayers. I would pray for Susie's recovery, and then I would ask God, that if was His will to take her home, that He be merciful and not let my dear wife suffer any longer. As hard as it was to imagine life without her, it was pure torture to see her the way she was. I was living a scenario that wasn't supposed to occur for many more years, and even then she was supposed to outlive me. Yet, here we were. I had even told her goodbye the night before while she was still in ICU. I whispered in her ear that if she wasn't with us the next morning, that I loved her and that I had a ball. I told her that if God was asking for her, then stop fighting and take His hand. It was the most difficult words I had ever spoken; yet, I felt better after I had said them.

When I got to room 442, I stopped suddenly before I opened the door. There was noise coming from inside her new room. It was loud, and it was happy! I opened the door slowly, my heart pounding. There was family surrounding Susie's bed, and from the entrance all I could see was Susie's feet. Someone said, "Susie, Rick's here!" and then they motioned for me to come in. I walked forward, and when I looked at Susie, her eyes were open, and she looked directly at me and smiled! Squeals of delight and cheers all around. I remained stoic. It was the wall I had built. I would not be lured out of it yet. I could not take any more ups and downs and keep my sanity. I went to her and whoever was on my side of the bed, the same side as in the ICU, made room for me. I picked up her still unmoving hand, leaned over her and kissed her.

"Well, good morning sweetie," I said. "Welcome back. I missed you. Can you hear me?" Susie stared at me, her smile remaining. Then I asked, "You think you could blink your eyes if you can hear me?" At that exact moment, her eyes closed and opened. More cheers and squeals, clapping as well. Susie looked all around, her smile about to crack that beautiful face of hers. This time I grinned, and even laughed out loud. Relief began to flood out of me like a dam bursting. Jimmy was directly across from me at Susie's bedside. He looked straight at me.

"So, are you better now? Have you got your attitude straight?"

The room was suddenly quiet. Jimmy's wife, Carla, elbowed him in the side. I couldn't believe it. I looked him in the eye. I kept my voice civil, and I told him, "Jimmy, don't you ever question what I want for this girl!" Nothing further was said. Susie quickly became the center of attention once again.

Everyone stayed a little while longer, then one by one began to leave. Susie entertained us with her smiles and blinks, and we were as happy as we had been for a long time.

Eventually, I was all alone with her. She was getting sleepy by now. That was fine with me. I would say her name, and her eyes would open. When she looked at me, there was not only recognition, but there was love as well. I would kiss her on the lips over and over, and I began tearing the wall down that I had built for protection. My hopes began to soar, and no matter how many times I told myself not to do it, brick by protective brick, the wall began tumbling down. I talked with Susie. I told her how glad I was to see her. I promised to bring all the kids in to see her. I talked about our business and how everyone was helping keep it going for us. I combed her hair and put Vaseline on her lips. Her forehead felt hot, so I put a cold towel on it. Her ever-present cough was as bad as ever, and I learned to suction her throat myself. She would fight it, but I stayed persistent and eventually would be successful. I didn't realize it at the time, but it was the beginning of learning how to take care of Susie, tending to her every need. In a way, we were witnessing a birth - a rebirth of sorts. Susie had come back to us, to me. I would take care of her the way I would take care of a newborn baby. I would feed her, bathe her, change her and clean her up, clear her throat and wipe her nose, help her get dressed, teach her to walk and talk, teach her to read and write, read to her and celebrate each and every new milestone she achieved. At times it was devastating to see her reduced to having to start over, but I would remind myself that we had very nearly lost her. Any part of Susie was better than nothing. I had to learn patience. I would learn to count my blessings.

I had awoke that morning believing that Susie might die. Three hours later I knew she would live.

For the second time since her heart attack, I had hope.

CHAPTER TWELVE:

A KISS
A NURSE
THE FEVER

I couldn't help but let my mind wander from time to time. I have heard of cases like this where, after surviving the heart attack, other parts of the body shut down.

Could this be happening to Susie?

E verybody remembers his or her first kiss.

It marks the beginning of a passionate relationship. The event is so special that couples who have been married for fifty years and more can recall it so vividly that it is as clear as if it happened yesterday. I remember our first kiss. It was a goodnight kiss on our first date. We had gone to my brother Mitch's house to eat dinner with him and his wife, Sandy. They had invited us as sort of an icebreaker date. We had a good time.

I took her home, next door to my house, and we talked outside in the carport for a long time. I was trying to get my courage up, and I think she probably knew it. She was so young, incredibly beautiful and I wanted to kiss her so badly I could taste it. Finally I got close enough and went for it. I needn't worry. She kissed me back as if she had fully expected it and wanted me to kiss her. My heart was beating out of my chest. I was in! I looked her in the eye, and in my sexiest voice, I said, "So, sweet thing, how about another date?"

"Sorry," she said, "I have a boyfriend."

Direct hit! Down in flames! Crash and burn!

I went home, feeling lousy. I later learned that she was just playing hard to get. She wanted me. It was either that or my continuous cards, letters, poems, songs, phone calls, flowers, stalking and harassment finally paid off. Many more kisses followed, her boyfriend was forgotten, and I married the girl of my dreams.

I wonder how many couples are fortunate enough to experience a second "first kiss"? It happened to me, but this time I never saw it coming. Susie and I were alone in her new room, the first afternoon she was in there. I was sitting by her side when she began coughing. Ready with the suction tube, I was finally able to clean out her mouth. Afterward she was wide-awake, staring directly at me. I know how much she hated that suction. I told her I was sorry, then wiped her mouth with a clean towel. I had kissed her countless times on the lips once her breathing tube had been removed, and I leaned over her to do it again. This time, however, she kissed me back!

Oh, man! She had pursed her lips and returned my kiss! I was so shocked I thought maybe I had imagined it. I looked at her and said, "Do that again!" I kissed her, and just like I asked her, she kissed me, too! How many thousands of times had this so very simple act occurred over the last 23 years? Susie was always fun to kiss. That second first kiss, though, that was the granddaddy of 'em all.

I don't know how many people I called. It was such an incredible milestone. It was not too long ago that I just knew I would never feel her lips kiss me again. This proved to me that she knew who I was. I experienced the same euphoria that I felt so many years ago in her parent's carport. The same goosebumps. This kiss in the hospital, this first kiss, filled me with hope. Once again, I felt I could look forward to a life with Susie. All because of one kiss.

This kiss occurred during her first day in the Acute Care ward. Susie's room was next to the nurse's station, one of only two rooms that were. One entire wall was nothing but windows. These rooms were reserved for those patients who were gravely ill, and the windows gave the nurses a 24/7 view of the patient. There were Venetian blinds on the windows, and eventually I would close them for privacy as long as I was in the room. She was still hooked up to heart monitors - the window view was more for choking or rolling out of bed, neither of which, at this point, was possible.

So I was feeling pretty good about things, the way anyone would feel after their first kiss. All in all, a pretty good start in Susie's new home.

It was also on this first day that Susie and I would meet

Brenda. One of the true silver linings to come from Susie's heart attack was Brenda. Without question, she was one human being who epitomized everything good about nursing. I believe she was a nurse's aid, or nurse's assistant, because she never gave shots or ordered medicine. But anything else, and I mean anything, was never a problem for her.

She was the kind of nurse that patients fall in love with. She was always happy. She was always smiling. She was the only nurse who, every time she walked in the room, got a smile out of Susie on sight. Susie would even let her put the "yonker" in without a fuss. (The yonker was Brenda's word for the suction tube. I never asked where she came up that name, but it stuck, and that's what it was called for the rest of Susie's hospital stay.)

There was never a task that Brenda was called on to do that even remotely resembled something she didn't care for. It didn't matter what it was, Brenda was more than happy to do it. Whether it was cleaning up a mess, changing bedding, moving Susie to a chair or back into her bed, taking her temperature, cleaning Susie up - whatever. She always made you feel like she was glad you needed her. I don't mean to give the impression that any of the other nurses who cared for Susie weren't anything but wonderful - they all were. But Brenda was special.

She would walk into the room the same way whether she was just coming on her shift or had already worked 12 hours. She was about Susie's age, maybe a little younger, medium height and build, and had a voice that had a country twang to it. Her energy level was phenomenal. She would walk in, fly around and do everything she came in to do, have a conversation with everyone in the room, and then be gone before the dust had settled. You couldn't help but like her. I can't imagine her having an enemy in the world.

We were there for a long time so we got to know each other

pretty well. She had two children I believe, and one baby grandson. She brought the baby to see us one Saturday. Susie has always loved babies, and she grinned from ear to ear when Brenda brought this one to see her.

Brenda began taking care of me as well. We had only been there a couple of days when she brought in a food tray. Susie was still on a nasal feeding tube and couldn't swallow a thing. I told Brenda this. "Oh, no, Rick, I bet she could eat this." She put the food on a roll around table and took the cover off the plate of food. It looked delicious.

"Brenda," I said, "she can't eat anything."

She never stopped what she was doing. She then rolled the table directly in front of me and said, "I bet somehow or other Susie manages to eat this all up! What do you think?" She winked at me. I finally caught on.

"You know," I said, winking back, "I bet she can, too." And you know what? *Susie* ate every bite.

Brenda noticed how often I was with Susie. I remained by her side ten to twelve hours a day during the week, and then 24 hours over the weekends. I left her only to be with the kids at night and to make sure our business was open and running every morning. Other than that, I was with Susie. Brenda saw this, and was moved. One night she told me something I will never forget.

"Rick, you know I'm getting married again because of you two."

"What?" I said. I couldn't imagine where this was going.

"You see, there's this guy who has been bugging me to marry him for a couple of years now. I been putting him off. Watching you guys, I'm gonna call him and tell him I'm ready."

I didn't get it. "How did watching us change your mind?"

"Because, if I'm ever sick like Susie is, I want someone to take care of me the way you take care of her."

I am always amazed when people tell me something like this. It never occurred to me to do things any differently than the way I did. I had to be with Susie. I didn't feel I warranted praise for doing the only thing I could do. I was flattered, and I was happy that I could make a difference in such an important decision. "Well, thanks, Brenda, I appreciate that." was all I could think to say. In those days, any bit of good news and good feelings were always welcome.

The first weekend in room 442 was long and difficult. Susie developed a fever late Friday night and couldn't shake it. Tylenol would help but not for long. A fever is a scary thing for patients as sick as she was. It could mean an infection somewhere in her body, and in her already considerably weakened condition, this could be dangerous.

Susie would still wake up. In fact, she had great difficulty sleeping. She would doze off for no more that a minute or two at a time, then wake up in obvious distress. This was how she lived for the entire weekend. It was miserable for me, and the rest of her family, to watch her like this, especially after the wonderful day Friday. It was always hard to take even the smallest step backwards. I knew she still wasn't completely out of the woods, but I was convinced she would live and recover. She had kissed me again. She would recover.

The nights were the hardest. I would roll the cot out and prepare the bed for sleeping. But I would learn that sleep would not be possible. From the time I woke in my own bed on Friday morning until I lay back down in this same bed Sunday night, I might have gotten two hours sleep. Susie was so miserable, however, that I never thought about my own exhaustion. I was much too worried for her. She wanted to sleep; I knew that. I could see it in her pitiful eyes. But she was burning up from fever; there was a tube running from her nose, down her throat and into her stomach; she had oxygen pouring into her nose from a tube underneath it, and the relentless coughing up phlegm and the inevitable suction afterward made sleep impossible. Jenny and I had asked the doctors to discontinue any medication that would dull her senses, and that would include pain medicine. By Saturday night, however, I was begging them for something that would help the poor girl get some rest. I didn't care if the sedative prolonged Susie's mental recovery, something that we were all so very anxious to know about. I was convinced that the complete lack of rest was far more detrimental. The nurses agreed, and administered the drug. Finally, Susie got some sleep.

I didn't, however. I would lie down, but every time she made the slightest noise I was up and making sure she was OK. I would put some fresh cold water on a towel and try to cool her forehead, face and neck. She would open her eyes briefly when she would feel the cold on her burning skin, and I would talk to her. She couldn't respond vocally, but I know she was telling me through her eyes that she was glad I was there. Then her eyes would close, and she would try to sleep. Her breathing was still the hardest thing to get used to. I could always tell when she was about to cough. Her breathing would sound a little like gargling, and as the phlegm would build, the gargling sounds would become louder. She would wait until the last possible breath before she would give in and cough. The coughing would be loud, prolonged and horrible. I would suction; it was the only time she looked at me with what could only be described as contempt, and her breathing would calm somewhat. But the never-ending cycle would begin again. It was by far one of the worst by-products of her illness. I longed for her agony to end.

I finally gave up any hope of sleeping at around 4:00 Sunday morning and went and found a cup of coffee. I took it back to the room and drank in relative silence. Susie had been given something for her fever an hour or so earlier and she was, at least for the time being, resting comfortably. We still didn't know what was causing her fever and I was worried. Some blood had been drawn for the infectious diseases doctor, but we wouldn't know the results for some time. Brenda had told me bacteria existed in every hospital that was immune to antibiotics, merely by being around these antibiotics all the time. From time to time they infect the patients and alternative treatment methods have to be used. But they first have to be identified. They don't infect everyone, but when fever like the one Susie had was prolonged and persistent, there was reason to worry. We would wait and see what the infectious diseases results were. Again, the ever present fear of the unknown.

I couldn't help but let my mind wonder from time to time. I had heard of cases like this where, after surviving the heart attack, other parts of the body shut down. Could this be happening to Susie?

The morning consisted of many more cups of coffee, cold towels on Susie's forehead, Vaseline on her lips, nurses in and out and the ever present fever. The hours went by. Around 8:00 her dad called to check on her. I told him there wasn't much change. He said he would be there in a half hour or so and then I could leave and take the kids to mass. I really didn't want to leave her, but what her dad was telling me was, "Rick, leave and take the kids to mass." He was right, of course. I needed to be with my children, and what better place to be with them and to pray for their mom than church? The logic was hard to escape.

The mass went smoothly until the homily. For you non-Catholics that would be the message from the priest. It's the part I look forward to the most. Instead of our usual priest, however, there was a guest priest who stepped up to the pulpit. He began talking about husbands and wives and the relationships they enjoy. I'm serious. I listened for a couple of minutes and then I had to leave. Obviously, he couldn't have known about Susie. And if she had been there with me we would have enjoyed it along with all the other couples in mass that morning. But Susie was lying in a hospital bed, racked with fever, and still very, very sick. I left my kids in the church and went outside. I walked around for fifteen minutes or so then rejoined my family inside. The homily was just over, and the offering plate was being passed around. There is a custom of mass where we pray for all those sick in the hospital and unable to attend. I knew Susie's name was on this prayer list, but I wasn't prepared for the shock of hearing it. When her name was called out, I nearly lost it. I felt my whole body shudder, and I had to hold on to the back of the pew in front of me to remain standing.

When it was time for communion I made sure I was in the line with the priest in it. When he offered the Body of Christ, I took the wafer and then leaned toward him and whispered in his ear, "Father, my wife is very, very sick. Could you please pray for her?" The tears were there now, and I heard him say, "I know son, I know." I didn't know if he really knew or not. I hoped he would say a prayer for her. When I got back to my seat, I found myself crying. Scotty would ask me later why I was crying at church. I told him I was just really worried about Mommy.

I don't think the priest even remembered my mentioning Susie during communion. As we left church that morning, I shook his hand. He never said a word. I was disappointed.

I took the kids home after church. They all had plans with various friends and family, and I was glad that they could enjoy a day away from the hospital. They would derive no pleasure from seeing their mother the way she was right now. I drove back to see Susie, hoping I could see even a microcosm of improvement. When I entered her room I was surprised to see only her mom and dad there. I asked how she was doing and they responded that there was little change. I went to Susie, held her hand, and talked softly to her. She was asleep, and I was glad to see her resting.

After only a few minutes I noticed that she had perspiration across her forehead. I felt her cheeks; she was burning up. I went over to the sink, found a clean towel, and wet it down. I began dabbing the cold cloth on Susie's forehead and cheeks. She immediately responded to the contrast between her hot skin and the cool towel. Her head moved away from me, but I continued to dab.

"Jesus Christ, Rick, why don't you just let the poor girl sleep?" her dad angrily said to me.

I knew then and there that things weren't right with myself and Susie's family. I had noticed that Jimmy was never there when I was. I was hoping that it was just bad timing. But now I knew for sure. To be fair, it was not her entire family. But Mac, Wanda and Jimmy, at least for now, with the memory of the stomach tube still fresh in their minds, considered me no longer a real part of their family. I had already taken Susie off DNR status: Do Not Resuscitate. I had put this on her chart right after the meeting in the chapel. If her heart had stopped again at that early stage I would not have allowed any Harvey Team heroics on her. Her family had agreed to this, but they did not agree with me that a stomach feeding tube was life support. And even though it looked as if I would not have to make this decision after all, they could not get over the fact that I had even entertained the idea of letting Susie go. I looked at Mac, the towel still on Susie's head, and sighed. I kept my voice low, but steady and deliberate, and said, "Mac, I'm just trying to help her."

"Oh, bullshit, Rick!"

"Mac," I said, "I really don't want to fight with you."

"Oh, Rick," he said, "there wouldn't be any fight." Right then Wanda let Mac know that it had gone far enough with a "Mac!" warning. I continued cooling Susie, unshaken by his threat. I had gone through too much at this point to let him bother me. They both left within a few minutes.

To be fair to Mac and Wanda, they had already buried one daughter, some 35 years earlier. Their first daughter, Lisa Marie, the one we named our daughter after, had died of Leukemia when Susie was about five. I understood that perhaps memories of this horrible time were being relived, and the thought of burying another child seemed incomprehensible. And Jimmy, I believe, was being haunted by advice he gave us the day of Susie's heart attack. If she had died I don't know if he could've handled it. Still, as bad as they were hurting, they could not comprehend my own pain.

I had a conversation similar to that last thought with Jan. It was only a day or two after Susie's heart attack and she was in terrible pain. Susie is her only sister and she was at the hospital as many hours as I was. She said to me, "Rick, I can't stand the thought of losing her."

"I know what you mean Jan," I said, "but can you imagine how I feel?"

"I promise you, Rick, that you can't possibly feel any worse than me. Susie is the only sister I have. If I woke up tomorrow and she wasn't here, I don't know what I'd do."

I didn't try to explain it to her then - I wasn't in a "I hurt worse than you do" argument mood, and that wasn't her intent anyway - but she couldn't have been more wrong. Susie was my life! Susie and Jan were sisters, buddies. They loved each other the way sisters do. But Susie and I were inseparable. We were a team. My whole world consisted of Susie on one side of me, my kids on the other. If Susie had died, every other person in the world would go on with his or her lives virtually unchanged. They would be sad, some devastated. Yet, their core world would remain virtually the same. My world would have been shattered. My four children would have remained with me, but understand that they are one half of my being, and Susie is the other half. I don't mean to minimize what my kids mean to me, but clearly Susie alone equals the sum of the other four. I'm sorry, but Susie was here first. Truly, this is love. This is the same love that made it easy to decide not to let them put a tube in her stomach. I literally didn't care what anyone else thought of me. The only thing I cared about was lying in front of me, ill beyond words. I would take care of her the best I knew how.

Susie remained very sick for the rest of that Sunday. She did not smile or respond to me, or anyone else, because of her fever. Brenda explained it to me. "What kind of mood are you in when you run 101 temperature?" I couldn't help but feel the pangs of worry, however. By the time Jan got there to spend the night with her late Sunday evening, I was exhausted and devastated. After her miraculous wakening Friday, she had been virtually unresponsive the rest of the weekend. I tried to remain upbeat, but it was difficult. I told Jan to take good care of her, and I went home nearly spent.

Because of the grace of God, though, Sunday night would be the last night I would spend not knowing if Susie would make it or not. The rest of her hospital stay would be spent wondering how much recovery there would be, not if she would recover. The roller coaster was still moving, but the uphill climbs were not as severe or as scary, and the downhill rides were smooth and very, very cool. Each improvement in her condition was a miracle. I began to describe Susie as one who would look at every doctor and nurse and, once they said she would never be able to do such and such, she would say, "Oh, yeah? Watch me!"

So we watched. And, my, did she put on a show!

CHAPTER THIRTEEN:

THE FIRST WORDS
THE FIRST STEPS

" *and then she said, 'Hi, Momma.'*"

The next morning, Monday morning, I returned to work for the first time since Susie's heart attack.

I had been to our cleaners two or three times before, but only to enter some deposits, catch up on some paperwork and just to look around the place. How it had changed since Susie had gotten sick. It just didn't mean the same to me. This was our business. It was never meant to be run by only me. As hard as I tried, I just couldn't motivate myself to feel the same way about it. If Susie had died, there is no way I would've kept the place. It was extremely difficult being there without her. I had a tough time trying to care. I didn't want to be there, but there had to be a point in time where I had to get on with other important aspects of my life. I owed it to Susie and the kids to keep our dream alive. My brother-in-law had to get back to his own business as well. When I called him the night before and told him I would be back the next morning, he made it clear that he would be there for as long as I needed him to. It was time, I told him. It was time. I thanked him for taking care of it for us.

I arrived at the cleaners early - before 5:00 in the morning. Extended sleep remained hopeless. I began going through the motions of preparing for the day. I counted the shirts, separated the darks from the lights and started the machines. I turned the boiler and the air compressor on. I got the drawer money out of the safe and put it in the register. I made coffee. I prepared a load of dry cleaning, put it into the cleaning machine, and started it. I got all of the spotting done. I did all of the things I had been doing for most of my working life. I kept waiting for the "Man, it's good to be back!" feeling, but it was not to be. There was one huge missing piece of the puzzle. Susie would not be pulling up in the back at 8:00 the way she had done for the last two years. Her cheerful "good morning!" would not resonate through the plant as she walked up front to mark in, her tea in one hand and normally an armload of personal clothes in the other. I was there in person, but certainly not in spirit. Not without Susie.

Customers began to arrive, and I began to find that, at least for a while, trying to get things done would be impossible. As soon as they saw I was back they would, understandably, inquire about Susie. I told the story about her condition so many times I doubt if the text changed more than a few words from customer to customer. They were all concerned and I was very moved. This was one of the reasons we never considered opening more that just this one location. This was a true family owned, mom and pop store. We were always there, and we got to know nearly all of our customers. Susie was always up front and the clientele loved her. What was not to love?

It was the same with the employees. They had no idea I would be there, and, of course, there was a reunion of sorts. Naturally they asked about Susie. I told them about her unbelievable Friday, and then about the fever over the entire weekend. It's not easy, I told them, going through the ups and downs of her recovery, but we have time. It would be a waiting game from this point on. Wait and pray.

I found I hadn't forgotten anything and the morning progressed smoothly. I called Jan, and she said that Susie had a restless night but had been actually sleeping pretty well for two or three hours. I was glad to hear it, and I told her to call me for anything or any change. I went back to hanging loads, loading and unloading washers, talking to customers and trying to stay busy so the hours would pass. I would only stay until the last load was in the machine and I could leave it with my employees to finish. I would leave for the hospital and Susie at the earliest possible moment.

It was about 9:45 when I thought I heard the phone ring. I was back by the steam tunnel, a noisy piece of equipment that pre-steamed garments before going to the presses. I took the

cordless out of my pocket and looked at it. If the phone had
been ringing, someone had answered it. I nearly put it back in
my pocket, but for some reason I hit the "talk" button. Sure
enough, I heard voices, and one of them was Jan's. I caught
the tale end of a sentence: "….. and then she said 'Hi,
Momma'."

My heart was pounding. I mean jackhammer, cannonball
pounding. I interrupted. "Wait a minute, Jan. Start over from
the beginning."

"Rick," she squealed, "she woke up! She looked right at
me, and I said hi to her, and then I swear to God she said hi
back to me! I almost died! And then I said, 'Susie, Momma's
here, say hi to Momma, and she looked at Momma and said
'Hi, Momma!'"

I sat down on the chair beside me. I could barely breathe.
"Jan, are you sure? She talked to you?"

"Yes, Rick, it was plain as day!"

"I'm on my way!"

I ran up front to find Lisa. "Lisa, your mom talked! I have
to go!" The poor girl wanted to go, too, but there was no way
both of us could leave. I told her as soon as she could get
someone to work for her, she could come to the hospital as
well. I absolutely flew to the hospital. It was only about five
miles from our cleaners so I was there in minutes. By the time
I got to her room I was completely out of breath. I ran from
where I parked to her room at a full gallop, and then took the
stairs three or four at a time. I walked in to a room full of people. Susie was bright-eyed, full of smiles and entertaining
everyone. Jenny was so excited she could barely contain herself. "Rick, come here, look at this!" She was holding a
white, plastic chalkboard. "How are you?" was written on it.
She said, "Rick, I wrote these words on here and held it up to
Susie. Rick, she read them! Plain as day, she read them!"

"I'm a witness, Rick," Jan said, "I heard her." Jan had been crying tears of joy, that much was plain. Her eyes were red and she had a tissue in her hand. Her mom and dad were there as well. I went to my side of the bed, and, as always, held her hand. She looked at me, eyes wide open. I leaned over her and kissed her. Again, as she would pretty much from then on, she kissed me back. I spoke to her, softly. I said, "Hey, sweetie. I hear you're talking to us." She smiled but didn't say anything. I tried again. "Susie, can you hear me?"

"Uh-huh." It was a whisper, barely discernable, but I heard her. I put my face into her pillow. The joy that filled my entire body was beyond description. I quickly regained my composure and spoke to her again.

"Do you know me?"

"Uh-huh."

"What's my name?"

"Rick Jacobs."

Communication, pure and simple. Her voice was not what I remembered. It was a very throaty, horse, sore, whispery voice, very low and very soft. In order to hear her at all, you had to be right by her. As strange as her voice sounded, it was beautiful to hear. We had been faced with the very real possibility that she would never communicate with anyone ever again, and yet here she was, answering questions and telling her momma hi! Her voice responding to questions was beyond my wildest expectations at this point.

Her reading the words that Jenny had written was another huge step towards mental recovery. For her to recognize letters was one thing - to be able to put them into words and read them was another. This took an enormous amount of brain function, and there was no question that she had read them.

How things had changed! Just three days earlier I was convinced that Susie would not recover beyond a vegetative state, and had prepared myself for this probability. The entire weekend had been spent with high fever and unresponsiveness.

And yet now, as I held her hand and looked at my wife, it all seemed a distant memory. She was talking with us! The relief I felt was immeasurable. I suddenly said, "Jan! I need to get the boys! They need to see this!"

"That's a good idea, Rick. What about Scotty?"

"Especially Scotty," I said. "I think it would do him, and Susie, a world of good."

"Have you taken a picture of her yet?" I hadn't. We had come up with the idea earlier of taking a Polaroid of Susie and letting Scotty see it before actually bringing him to see her. He would see the nose tube and wires on her chest beforehand, and we hoped it would lessen the shock. He had not seen her at all since her heart attack. We got the camera out and took the picture. Susie wouldn't smile for us, but the picture turned out well. It showed clearly the way Susie looked. Jan volunteered to get the older boys, and we left the hospital.

I checked Scotty out of school and, once we were back in the car, I showed him the picture of his mom. He stared at it for a while and I let him take his time. Finally, he asked me, "Do those wires hurt Mommy?"

"No, son, they don't. Nothing hurts her anymore."

"Why is that thing in her nose?"

"It's how she eats."

"Food goes in that little wire?"

"It's a tube, son. And the food is like chopped up real good, and it goes down that tube and into her stomach."

"Does it taste good?"

I laughed. "I don't think she can taste it." Then I got serious. "Scotty, don't be afraid of all the wires and tubes. They are all there to help Mommy get better. She's doing a lot better now, and that's why I can take you to see her. She even talked a little today. Are you ready?"

"Yes, sir! I been ready!"

"OK, big guy, let's go!"

Scotty would cling to that picture for weeks, until Susie was home for good. He was proud of it. He would show it to his friends. "This is my mommy!" he would proudly say. Taking that picture was a great idea. I was glad we thought to do it.

I was anxious to see how Scotty would react to seeing his mother for the first time in nearly two weeks. He and Susie had always been very close. Even with the picture to prepare him, I wasn't sure how much shock there would be to see his mother live and wired. I needn't worry, though. He walked into that room and straight up to Susie. She looked at him, smiled, and said, "Hi, Scotty."

That was all he needed. He climbed into the bed with her, gave her a hug and a kiss, and then snuggled against her as if they were home and in our own bed. She had said his name and smiled at him, and it was as if all of the tubes and wires had magically dissolved. He was careful not to hurt her. He instinctively knew to be very careful around her. It was great to see.

The other boys were treated to their names being said out loud as well. Lisa joined us at the hospital very shortly after the boys had gotten there with Jan, and it was the whole family together again, the first time since the heart attack occurred. It was not how I pictured a family reunion - in a hospital room with Susie in bed and still very sick, and the kids and me surrounding her - but it was all right. What Susie had done today went beyond anything I had expected, and I was optimistic. I had reason to feel great hope again. Her heart was beating normally, and Dr. Weinstein was nothing but confident that it would continue to do so indefinitely. Her respiration was excellent; her oxygen level remained high, though we were still on nasal oxygen. Her temperature was finally down, and she had talked and read. What a morning!

Her condition would improve steadily over the next two

and a half weeks in the Acute Care ward. It was almost as if her talking was what put us over the edge and finally on the road to full recovery, at least physically. For a long time it was terribly difficult to understand Susie, her voice was so weak and her throat so sore from the breathing tube. I was always afraid she would give up trying to talk because we would be forced to ask her to repeat herself several times every time she would say something. I kept at her, though. I would tell her that the only way her voice would get stronger was to keep on talking. Never get discouraged, I said. And, God bless her, she didn't.

Almost as soon as she began to communicate with us we noticed that her arms and legs began to move. At first we were pretty sure it was involuntary movement, but then we began to notice some purposeful movements. This, of course, was huge. The left side of her body woke up long before her right side, and this was a little scary. I was so afraid of a stroke-like condition where one side would remain paralyzed. Her left arm and hand began to lift up and down, and I noticed her left leg would move a little. I got her to wiggle her toes on both legs, and this was very promising. Her wiggling her toes gave her some comfort as well.

I was with her one afternoon and we were alone. This was still early in the first week in the acute care ward. Susie was awake, and would talk to me in one and two word sentences. I don't recall exactly what I was doing, but I looked down at her and I noticed she had tears in her eyes. Then, out of the blue, she began to sob hysterically. I mean, she was crying her eyes out. This was the absolute first show of any emotion whatsoever that she had shown, and it appeared to be for no reason at all. I didn't know what to do. I asked her what was wrong. Of course, she couldn't answer. I tried to think. Why would she be crying? And all of a sudden, it hit me.

Susie had just begun to become aware again. She was

beginning to figure things out. Now she's lying here, and she can't move, or at least not very much at all. She thinks she's paralyzed! I quickly moved to the end of the bed and lifted the blankets off her feet and legs. "Susie, look at me!" She did. I lifted one of her legs and put her foot against my chest. I said, "Can you feel this?" I massaged her foot. She quit crying. I repeated, "Can you feel me massaging your foot?" She finally nodded. "Good! Good! Now, can you wiggle your toes for me?" Almost immediately, I felt just the slightest pressure against my chest from her toes. I was ecstatic! "Outstanding! Now, listen to me, sweetie, you are not paralyzed. You could not feel this, and you could not wiggle your toes if you were. You had a heart attack, and you are very, very tired. But we are going to get you stronger, you hear me? You will walk again! I promise, you will walk again!"

I waited. Susie stared at me as I kept massaging. I moved to her other leg and foot. "See, baby, you can feel that, can't you? You're getting out of this bed one day, count on it." Suddenly, she smiled. It was OK. I had guessed right.

I carefully put her leg back down and went around to her. I picked her hand up and sat on the edge of her bed. I looked at her, and I said, "Susie, no matter how long it takes, you'll never be alone. I'll be right here with you. You will get better, and then we'll pick up right where we were before this happened. One thing, though, we're not going to work as hard as we used to. This has taught me one thing - slow down and enjoy life. I didn't think we would have any more time, but you're gonna be fine."

She didn't take her eyes off me; she didn't even blink. I could tell, I mean I just knew she understood every word I was telling her. "You really scared me, you know that, don't you? I was never meant to be alone, you know. You better be glad you're going to make it."

Right then, she did the most amazing thing. I had her left

126

hand, but she lifted her right hand and pointed toward her right shoulder. "What do you want me to do?" I asked her. She kept pointing. "You want to tell me something?" I leaned down and put my ear beside her mouth. It was then I felt her hands move across my back, very slowly and very deliberately. It took almost a superhuman effort on her part, but finally she accomplished what she wanted to do. She hugged my neck. When I realized what she was doing, I just about lost it. It was as special as the first kiss, as meaningful as her first words, and so unspeakably comforting to me. I carefully put my arms underneath her, and cradled her, holding her as tightly as I dared, and we remained in each other's arms for several minutes. Happily, no one entered the room during this extremely tender moment, and for a while no one else and not one other thing in the world mattered. Until that wonderful time, I had not seen her move her arms more than a few inches, and her right arm even less. But, somehow, she found the strength and the will to move them for me. It remains one of the most deeply moving moments of my life.

Once her arms began moving, man, they got busy. Her main mission in life became imminently clear: Remove the nasal feeding tube. Get that tube the hell out of my nose! This is exactly what she would have said to us had she been able to talk better. The instant she became aware of it, she hated the thing. It was a continual struggle, a never-ending battle fought between her and whoever happened to be in the room with her at any given time. Her left arm would begin to move, then slowly slide upwards, as if to imply, "Nothing going on here. Don't you pay me no mind at all. Just scratching my nose is all I'm doing." But, inevitably, the hand would reach for the tube. I would usually let her get almost to it. I wanted her coordination to get all the practice it could. A couple of times my attention wandered for a minute, and she actually grabbed it and began pulling. But every time I would take her hand and stop her.

Uh, did I say every time?

There was one Saturday night; It was the second weekend in the new unit that I stayed with her. She was really starting to come around now, and her hatred for the nasal tube was obvious. She would not leave it alone. I fought with her, begged her to go to sleep, but every few minutes she would wake up and up the hand would go. I was afraid to lie down. Her eyes would close and I would watch her. Just when I was about to lay down, the hand would begin to move. Finally, about 3:00 a.m., I moved the cot parallel with her bed and I put my hand on top of hers through the safety rail. I laid down beside her, her hand safely in mine, and fell sound asleep.

It was a couple of hours later when I heard a nurse say, "Oh my God, what have you done?" I knew exactly what had happened. I sat up and looked at Susie. She was sound asleep, the nose tube was out, her "food" was spilled all over her, and she looked more peaceful than I had seen her in a long time. She had gotten her hand out of mine and I never knew it. I must have been more tired than I thought. I asked the nurse if she had to put it back in. She said yes. "Can't it wait? Can we not see if she can eat?"

"We have to have a swallow test first," she said.

"Then give her a swallow test."

"Her doctor has to order one. I'll see about that Monday, but until then the tube has to go back in."

"Not yet," I said, "Let her sleep. She won't starve. Besides, I don't want to be here when you do it to her again. I don't want to see it." Her nurse left without putting it back in.

My relief showed up, and I left to take my kids to church. When I got back to the hospital the tube was back in and Susie looked miserable. I was, too. Jenny was there. She said, "Rick, we can get the tube out."

"How?"

Nov. 14, 1980. Susie still looks the same. Most of my hair has disappeared though. Who picked out that tux?

This was us in 1998 with Chip and Beth at our lakefront property. Many wonderful weekends were spent there together.

My parents, Pike and Marilyn Jacobs, in front of their dream in Daytona Beach.

"The Girls" on one of their trips to Daytona. From left to right: Susie, my sister Becky, Dad, my sister-in-law Sandy, and my sister Terri.

The entire family on the front counter of our business. The figure on the door to the right is a halloween decoration, not a customer.

Here we are with Scotty in front of our dream just a few months after we opened.

Susie and Lisa sometime before her heart attack. Can you tell where Lisa gets her good looks?

One of my favorite pictures with my baby girl!

Scotty's sixth birthday party, just seven days before Sept. 5th.

Susie and Beth the weekend before her heart attack.

While all the nurses were top notch, Scott Arthur was a large reason I was able to survive CVICU. In 2002, he was named one of the top 100 nurses in Shelby and Fayette County in Tennessee. No surprise there at all.

This was Susie's second "awakening" only nine days after her heart attack. Never did her smile look so good to me,

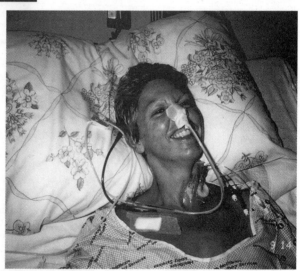

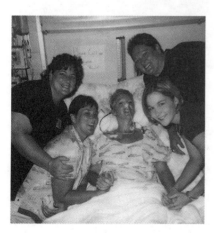

On one of her best afternoons in the Hospital, Susie thrilled (from left) Terri, her guardian angel Aunt Jenny, Lisa and Pam, a friend of the family.

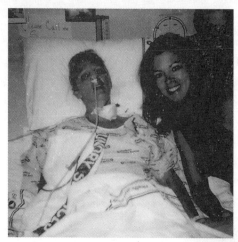

Again, during her second awakening, with her happy sister Jan and Wanda, her mom.

Here is Susie in her stroke chair and sunglasses, ready to be wheeled outside "442 is mobile!"

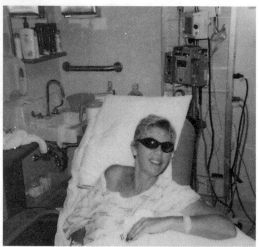

The "Honeymooners" at the Rehab Hospital. I had to hold her this way or she would fall, so we got the nickname.

Here we are, minus Scotty and Ricky and including Susie's mother Wanda, in the courtyard at the Rehab Hospital. Scotty must be taking the picture

Susie and Jan enjoying a moment at a Christmas party. Susie had been home two months.

This Excursion was her pride and joy for just a few short weeks. Believe it or not, it uses gas just sitting in the driveway with the ingnition off!

The Jacobs Family at the 2002 Family reunion. Susie is in the middle of all these folks. I'm the bearded one the back.

"We can allow the peg tube."

Of course! I couldn't believe I hadn't thought of it. They thought perhaps I was still against it. I was only against it if it were a permanent life support attachment. Absolutely put it in.

"My God, yes! When can they do it?"

"I've already asked them. If it's OK with you, they can schedule it for tomorrow."

"Tell me where to sign." And, the next day, it was in. There was nothing to it, really. A small hole was made, right next to her belly button, and about a one-quarter inch diameter soft plastic tube was inserted. The tube went directly into her stomach. On the other end outside, a large reservoir was attached. A funnel was used, and the liquid nourishment was poured into it. Gravity would cause the liquid to flow out of the reservoir, down the tube and into Susie's belly. None of the pleasure, but all of the necessary vitamins and minerals to sustain a healthy diet. The best part of all this was that the evil nose tube was gone forever. If Susie could have done back flips, she would have.

I wanted the swallow test. Her doctor was hesitant this early - there was a real danger that fluid would enter her lungs if her swallow and gag reflex weren't working properly. But Jenny and I had been working on this. We would bring tea or coke to her room, and then use some foam swabs to soak up the liquid. At first Susie didn't trust anything that was to be put in her mouth. She feared it was the yonker. Eventually, though, she relished the cold liquid that actually had taste to it. We were careful, but it was clear she was swallowing.

I knew for sure she could handle it on a beautiful afternoon outside the hospital. We had been transferring Susie to a "stroke chair," basically a recliner on wheels, for quite some time. She enjoyed leaving the room and especially loved going out into the fresh air. I had a pair of sunglasses she would put on and off we would go. I would leave the room with the announcement, "442 is mobile!" We had to let them know so they wouldn't freak when the heart monitor was out of range.

We had a special place we would go sit. Susie would watch the people and cars go by and realize there was still a world out there. On this particular afternoon, Lisa was with us. She had a Dr. Pepper in her hand. All of a sudden, Susie reached for the bottle. I told Lisa to let her have it. Susie held the bottle in one hand, and with the other attempted to twist the cap off. I was amazed. I was also unsure what to do. I asked her, "Do you want a drink?"

By now she was talking fairly well. "Well, duh!"

I laughed. "Do you think you can swallow it?" She had only drunk from the swabs prior to now. I didn't know what she would do with the bottle.

"Yes, I can swallow it." She was indignant. I took the cap off for her and held the bottle to her lips. I tipped it up ever so carefully, and as soon as the soda touched her lips, I quickly dropped it back down. I waited. There was no swallow. I panicked. "Swallow it, Susie!"

She said, "I would if I had gotten any in my mouth!" We all laughed, and this time I made sure the liquid entered her mouth. She swallowed it, made a face, and then wanted more. She took two or three more swallows without a problem.

I was thrilled! I had Lisa stay with her while I went and got her some sweet tea. She loves sweet tea more than she loves me. I put a straw in the cup and put it to her lips. She drank and drank, and swallowed and swallowed. I called one of the nurses in and had Susie demonstrate. Her nurse watched, and said, "I'm ordering the swallow test for first thing in the morning."

I went with Susie to her test. I had to wait outside while a nurse wheeled her inside the testing room. A machine x-rayed a liquid dye that Susie swallowed and determined whether it all went down into her stomach, or if there remained any danger of her choking. I stood right outside the room and listened closely. I soon heard, "Excellent, Susie, way to go!" from inside. I pumped my fist, and whispered a loud, "Yes!" The relief I felt was overwhelming.

Susie passed the swallow test and was immediately able to eat and drink anything she wanted. Her doctor let the peg tube remain for several weeks until he was sure she could eat enough to sustain her. Susie did just fine. She had very little trouble holding anything down.

One time, however, my sister, Terri, brought Susie some tater tots, one of her very favorite foods. They were both happily eating, and I was telling Terri a story about how a friend of mine's church had a special prayer session just for Susie. I said, "Terri, they had over 350 people show up, they all made a prayer chain, and one at a time, prayed for Susie. I mean, they didn't even know Susie, but still they did this for her."

I had forgotten how emotional Susie was now. She started sobbing from hearing this story, and then she began to choke. I immediately went to her, but the food refused to come up and she starting seriously gagging and choking, completely unable to take a breath. I panicked. I went around her and did a Heimlich maneuver on her. Well, it worked. All of the tater tots came pouring out of her mouth. What scared me was the blood that came up with it. I was mortified! "Get a nurse!" I told Terri. "Hurry!"

The nurses came rushing in. "There's some kind of bleeding," I told them. They assessed the situation, and then asked me if Susie had put ketchup on her tater tots. I said, sheepishly and with great relief, that she had. They laughed and then left. I imagine they will tell this story to their grandchildren. I guarantee I will.

Things were going extremely well now. Susie was progressing far beyond anyone's wildest dreams. In fact, the doctor had ordered the removal of some IV ports that had been put in her neck. This was great news because the location of the port was uncomfortable and irritating to Susie. A nurse came in to remove the port, and Jenny offered to assist. They both put on sterilized gloves, and I sat back to watch.

A tube several inches long was inserted into her skin when the port was first put in. When her nurse pulled this out of her, I was amazed by the length of it. I assumed it was just below the skin and into a vein. I'm not sure where it went, I didn't ask, and I was astounded when they removed it. It seemed routine enough. The port was removed, a bandage was readied, and then Susie, once again, seemed to die in front of me.

For no apparent reason, she began gasping for breath. It was terrifying. Susie made huge, deep, desperate attempts to get enough breath into her lungs, but it seemed the deeper she breathed, the more frantic she became. Panic shown in her eyes, clear and unbridled, as her breaths became more frequent and ineffective. Susie's skin turned an ashen color, almost gray. She was in grave danger, and all three of us knew it.

The most upsetting thing to me, again, was my utter inability to do anything for Susie. I simply stared, horror-struck that this could possibly be happening again. She was doing better! How in the hell could this be? Beyond my panic, it became obvious that the nurse removing the port was surprised by this unforeseen event, and looked confused and unsure of what to do.

Thank God for Jenny.

Immediately upon observing that the nurse was, at least temporarily, at a loss for what to do next, Jenny took over. Her fifteen years as an ER nurse came flooding back, and she began barking orders and giving instructions. She asked me to leave, and things began to happen all at once. I went outside and watched doctors, nurses and equipment flying in and out of her room. Dr. Weinstein was paged over the intercom to return to Susie's room, STAT! The pulmonary Harvey Team was paged to her room, STAT! I was surrounded by probably every nurse on the floor who wasn't in Susie's room, and they tried to comfort me. They assured me that the very best people in the hospital were with her. They tried to tell me not to worry. They brought me a glass of water. They put arms around me and never left my side.

I was inconsolable, however. This could not be happening! Susie was getting better, not worse. What I saw in there was a person who could not breathe. She could still *die*? That thought hadn't entered my mind in such a long time. We were out of the woods, weren't we? What was taking them so long? I imagined the bed would come flying out of the room and off to emergency surgery, or somewhere else where we would be starting all over, back to day one. I doubted I could take that again.

Finally, after twenty agonizing minutes, everyone came out. Dr. Weinstein came over to me, and said everything was fine. He wasn't sure exactly what had happened, but she was stable and suffered no adverse effects whatsoever. I could go see her now.

I went in and she looked fine. I hugged Jenny and thanked her for saving Susie's life. Jenny later told me she thinks the port had accidentally punctured part of Susie's lung when it had been originally put in. I remembered the physician who put it in had been afraid of that very thing, but an x-ray had shown negative. Jenny felt like, when the tube was removed, a blood clot had entered her lung. No permanent damage. No further danger. Just a scared husband, aunt and nurse.

Jenny got the ball rolling. Jenny was able to forget that Susie was family, and somehow get beyond this attachment and do what was necessary to save her life. I could never express the profound gratitude I feel for what she did for my family and me. She'll downplay it. Don't be fooled for a second. I was there, and I saw it. Jenny was the guardian angel that Susie so believes in.

This episode didn't slow Susie down at all. She was able to bounce back and continue to improve. I would, from time to time, take her down to the Cardiovascular ICU and visit with all her nurses there. They would gather around her and marvel at her progress. This always made her cry, and then the nurses would cry as well. It was good for them to see her. She was proof that miracles do happen.

One of the most moving incidents that happened while we were in the hospital occurred on her best friend's birthday. I told Susie that Beth was on her way and that she needed to sing happy birthday to her. Susie said she would, but I was dubious. She was still limited to short sentences, and I wasn't sure if she even knew the happy birthday song at this point.

When Beth arrived Susie was in the middle of a bath so Beth waited outside. We put a fresh gown on Susie and got her into the stroke chair. I wheeled her down to the elevators where Beth was waiting. As soon as Susie saw her, and without me saying a word, she began singing: "Happy birthday to you, happy birthday to you…" she looked at me as if puzzled. I whispered, "happy birthday dear Beth." That was all she needed. "Happy birthday dear Beth, happy birthday to you!"

Beth was absolutely stunned. And then the tears started. And then Susie's tears started. I asked Susie why she was crying. She said, "Because Beth is!" Good enough.

Susie's voice remained hoarse and rough. You could just barely hear the old Susie. The tune was barely recognizable. Yet, Beth would later tell me it was the best birthday present she had ever gotten in her life. And she meant it. As I wrote earlier, Beth and I had talked many nights out in front of my house when Susie was not expected to make it. Now, we were all here, and Susie had just sung happy birthday.

Once Susie was out of danger physically, and it was obvious she would recover, they began therapy on her. She was given therapy to strengthen her body, and improve her speaking, memory and alertness.

I'll never forget the first time Susie was able to sit up on her own. The therapist was thrilled. If Susie could balance, it was a major step towards walking.

The exercises Susie was put through were numerous and boring. It included lots of bending, moving, lifting and complaining, all of it from Susie. Her entire body was devastated from the heart attack, so I knew the therapy would be long and grueling. The physical end of all of this didn't concern me nearly as much as the mental side of it.

I had begun to notice that what Susie said, a lot of times, made no sense. I ignored it for the most part, thinking the drugs and the Dilantin were the culprits, and that this would improve as well. The physical improvements far overshadowed everything else. We were so deliriously happy with each and every milestone physically, that we assumed the mental capacity would return in time as well.

We assumed the key was the Dilantin. We had to get her off this drug. Dr. Weinstein, making his rounds one afternoon, promised he would talk to Dr. Pulan about getting her off of it completely. The next time we saw her, Dr. Pulan said she would order half doses for a day or two, then, if there were no seizures, she would order the drug stopped completely. The Dilantin would stay in her system for only a day or so after it was stopped, and then we would know.

She ordered another EEG, but told us the same thing she had told us the last time. There was less brain activity than before the brain swelling. This was still inconclusive - an MRI would tell us more. I wasn't worried yet. There was very little to indicate that Susie's brain was damaged. Sure, she said things occasionally that made little sense, but look what she had been through. Her brain would be fine. I was sure of it.

The Friday before we left the hospital we were paid a visit by Dr. Dale Cunningham. He was a doctor of therapy. He came into the room, introduced himself, and said, "Well, Mr. Jacobs, the therapists here tell me that Susie has really done well. I think she is a good candidate for aggressive therapy. We have a hospital in midtown that is perfect for her."

I looked at him. "You mean we can't keep doing the therapy right here?" I didn't want to go anywhere. This hospital was five minutes from our home.

He shook his head. "Oh, no. We don't have an inpatient facility here. She'll need to undergo inpatient therapy for several weeks, then we can discuss outpatient."

"Wait, hold everything Doc. We aren't having this conversation. You mean she won't go home from here?"

"No, Mr. Jacobs. I thought you knew. She'll check into our midtown rehabilitation hospital for probably anywhere from three to six weeks. She'll then need out-patient therapy for months, maybe years."

I was completely taken aback. I had no idea that Susie wasn't coming home from here. I thought we would be able to stay indefinitely, or at least continue on an outpatient basis. But now Dr. Cunningham told me it may be up to six weeks before I would have my wife home with me. It was a harsh reality. I managed to ask, "When will we leave here?"

"She's ready now, but we're having trouble with your insurance approving her stay. If we have to, I'll do it on a charity basis. I won't destroy your family's finances. I'll know more on Monday. In the meantime, we'll continue working with her here."

"What kind of a hospital is it where she'll be going? Can we stay with her at night?"

"Probably not, Mr. Jacobs. She'll have a roommate, and they really want her to begin to do things on her own. You'll have unlimited visitation during the day, but you'll have to leave her at night."

I was crushed. The thought of Susie not coming home for another three to six weeks seemed impossible to comprehend. It had already been more than five weeks. The loneliness I felt at night was beginning to overwhelm me, and it would be especially bad now, with her so far away and no one staying with her. I looked at her. She had no idea that we had been discussing her living arrangements for the next several weeks.

As always, I spent the weekend with her, the last weekend we would be there. She had a particularly good day Saturday, lots of therapy and lots of trips outside in between. Her spirits were high; she was talking a lot and eating like a horse. She was gaining strength and continued to amaze everyone there. I spent Saturday night with her and we both got a good night's sleep.

What happened Sunday morning could only be described as a miracle. I woke up about 5 a.m. and went and got some coffee. I drank it in her room and watched the news on TV with the volume down low. About six or so, she began to stir. I asked her how she felt. "I feel really good, Rick."

"Good," I said, "what would you like to do today?"

What she said next shocked me. "Rick, I really think I want to walk."

Really! I thought. What do I do? "OK, then let's walk."

I helped her up to a sitting position and brought her legs around to the side until her feet were on the floor. I sat down beside her and had her put her arm around me. I put my arm underneath her armpit for support and asked, "Well, you ready?" She said she was. "Then let's stand up."

I don't really know what I expected. But when I stood up, she stood up. This was the first time I had seen her on her feet in nearly six weeks, at least where she was actually standing. I was there for balance and to keep her from falling - she was doing the work. I said to her, "Now, do you think you can walk?" She nodded. "OK, sweetie, here we go then."

We took a step. Then we took another. We were walking! We walked around the end of the bed to the windows. The blinds were shut so no one could see the miracle going on inside the room. As we walked by, I knocked on the window like a mad man. I'm surprised I didn't break the glass. They must've thought something was wrong because, within seconds, there were three or four nurses coming through the door. Susie and I walked towards them. At first they were stunned. Then, they all cheered and clapped. Their "brain dead" patient in room 442 was out of bed and walking! I was so elated I could barely function. I had dreamed so many times, over and over the last few weeks, of walking with my wife again. And here we were, the dream coming true. We walked to a chair, and I carefully sat her down. She was grinning like a Cheshire cat, especially with all the nurses making such a fuss. I went straight to the phone and called everyone in the free world.

She ate breakfast in that same chair. What was so amazing is that this chair had no sides. She kept her balance during the entire time she ate her food. I was right there beside her, of course, but I never had to touch her. When she finished, we walked to the sink together and she brushed her teeth. I helped her to bed from there. By then her mom and dad had arrived and I went to get the kids for church.

It was the most glorious celebration I had ever experienced inside that church. I was so incredibly happy. What had made that woman of mine decide to want to walk I'll never know. It was beyond my wildest dreams. When I took communion I said to the priest, "Father, there has been a miracle! I'll tell you about it after mass." He couldn't wait for me to tell him. He was delighted to hear it.

Before the end of that Sunday, Susie and I had walked down to the end of the hallway outside her room. It was probably no more than 50 feet. I had Brenda follow us with a wheelchair, thinking Susie would tire before we got to the end, but she made it. She had an audience of nurses watching her, and they all clapped and cheered when she turned around and waved. The difference between Saturday and Sunday was night and day. If someone had tried to tell me that Susie would walk at all, much less that kind of distance, I would have suggested they commit themselves.

Before we would leave on the next Thursday afternoon, Susie was walking with a walker. On our last afternoon, we visited the CVICU one last time, only this time Susie walked in with only the walker assisting her. It was a great reunion. She truly was a miracle. And these wonderful, caring people had as much to do with her recovery as divine intervention did. The entire hospital had worked together to save my wife's life. When she had arrived four weeks and one day earlier, her heart was not beating and she was not breathing on her own. She had her hand out to God, and He was reaching for her. But, for some reason, He didn't take it right away. He had a reason for letting her stay.

We packed up everything in her room and, of course, went through all of the tearful goodbyes. An ambulance arrived to take Susie to the rehabilitation hospital, and she was strapped to a stretcher. As we walked out of room 442 for the final time, I looked around. I hoped the next occupant would have as successful a stay as we had.

We were on our way to the final chapter in Susie's recovery, at least inside hospitals.

CHAPTER FOURTEEN:

THE REHABILITATION HOSPITAL

I told myself that if she said, "Rick, I want to go home!" I would put her in my car and take her.

As I drove to the place where Susie would live for the next two weeks, I had mixed emotions. We were leaving the hospital, and wasn't that the goal from day one, to leave the hospital? She had been there four weeks and a day, and it had seemed much longer. Yet, I felt depressed.

For one, I had pictured her leaving with me, in our car, and then we would drive home to a huge reunion with family and friends. Instead, she was leaving the same way she arrived - in an ambulance. And she wasn't coming home. She was merely being transferred to a different hospital. A rehabilitation hospital that would help her gain strength, relearn simple skills and, hopefully, teach her how to take care of herself again. But couldn't I teach her that? I guessed, realistically, I didn't have the training. But I had watched her rehabilitation during the last few days and I could do what they were doing. I would watch her therapists at this new hospital as well.

The most devastating aspect was that she would have to live there - without family. She would even have a roommate. None of us could stay with her at night. As much as I hated leaving her every night to be with my kids before, at least I was comforted knowing there was a family member with her at all times. This was so different. I even had a suitcase in the backseat that I had to pack for her the night before. I cannot begin to describe how difficult it was packing that suitcase. I had to pack clothes, pajamas, underclothes, toiletries - everything she would need for an extended stay. It had to be one of the hardest, if not the hardest, tasks I had ever done.

It was also a twenty-minute drive from our home. That may not seem like a lot, but when I had been used to five minutes, it made a difference. I met families of patients while we were there that lived hundreds of miles away, however, and I learned to count my blessings.

I found the hospital. It was very nice from the outside, new and modern. There were plenty of parking spaces - quite a difference from the medical hospital - and I was able to park close to the front door. There was an ambulance parked right by the front entrance, and I guessed, correctly, that it was Susie's. I walked through the automatic doors and, with her suitcase in one hand and some hang up clothes in another, I went to the receptionist and asked for Susie's room. She told me room 210 and pointed to the elevator.

While I waited for the elevator, I looked around. The bottom floor was beautiful. There was a large lounge area with lots of comfortable seating and a color TV mounted next to the ceiling in one corner. It was immaculately clean and cheerful. Plants were in every corner and colorful paintings adorned the walls everywhere you looked. A sign next to the elevator advertised an orientation for new patients at 6:00 that same evening. That was only 20 minutes away. I made a mental note to be attend.

The elevator opened and I walked in. The doors closed and I noticed that when the elevator finally began it's upward journey, it seemed incredibly slow. There was very little of the jolt you feel in most elevators when it first takes off. The same thing when it stopped, very deliberate and drawn out. I surmised that a lot of the elevator riders in this hospital were rehabilitation patients, and most were weak and unstable on their feet. Sudden jerks could result in a fall. These elevators were specially designed for passengers with disabilities.

I arrived at the second floor, the ever present ache in my stomach a constant reminder of the fear and dread I was feeling. I had a suitcase and clothes in my possession, but Susie and I weren't going on a trip together. I was leaving her here, and I was going home alone, perhaps for an unbearably long time. Walking to her room, my worst fears were confirmed.

This place was no more than a nursing home!

All of the patients here seemed older than 70. The vast majority were in wheelchairs, the others barely able to walk with walkers. This hospital reminded me of most all of the other nursing homes I had ever been in. I despised nursing homes. I don't mean to prejudice all homes, but the ones I had experienced, either through business or visits, were horrible places where employees were untrained, uncaring and too few to properly care for the patients unfortunate enough to have to live there. These so called homes were also dirty and smelly, and most of the residents were too far-gone mentally to care. These places always depressed me, and the thought of my wife living here filled me with a sense of intense sorrow and resolve. She would not stay here a minute longer than she had to. I would rehabilitate her myself. If she seemed unhappy here, I would take her home.

When I found her room she was in bed and eating supper. Her mother was with her, as was her 93-year-old roommate. I kissed Susie, and asked her how she was doing. She said she was fine, then mentioned how good the food was. I had to admit it did look good. I saw there was a closet and a set of drawers for each patient and I started putting her clothes away for her. I tried to keep the mood light for Susie. I didn't want her to know that it was tearing me up inside, having to put her clothes and lingerie in this place and not at home. She seemed happy enough to be there. I didn't know if that would change when I had to leave and she would be alone.

I was surprised that her mom and I were the only ones there that first night. There were no other visitors at all. I guess the rest of our families figured we needed the time to ourselves to get used to the new surroundings and to get settled in. They were right, really.

Wanda and I went to the orientation. There was only one other person at the meeting other than the facilitator, and I was glad. We could ask all the questions we wanted and gained lots of valuable information. I was immensely relieved to know they had patients who were near Susie's age and some even much younger. We were told of a six-year-old girl who was there and that the oldest patient they ever had was 106!

They gave us the grand tour. I observed that the entire hospital was dazzlingly clean, a huge difference from nursing homes. Also, everywhere you looked were reminders that the patients there were there for one reason: to get better, stronger and well enough to go home, another distinction that comforted me. Nursing homes were places where people went to die. No one was here for that reason. Everyone was here to improve his or her quality of life!

The orientation ended. I had names and phone numbers of people who were in charge of Susie's care; I had seen the gym where Susie would exercise and get stronger, and I had seen the dining room where she would eat her meals. (There were no chairs in the dining room, and I was told that most patients ate from their wheelchairs. Not Susie, I thought to myself). The best news was, I was told that we would be given a target discharge date after Susie was evaluated the next day. That was excellent! We would know that soon at least an approximate date when she could go home to stay. Her 40th birthday was in a little over three weeks - that would be my personal target date.

Wanda left very shortly after the tour, leaving Susie and me in her room. She seemed to be handling it very well. She was still in the clothes that she had worn from the hospital and I assumed, correctly, that one of the floor nurses would help her change into her pajamas. It was good to know that she would never wear another hospital gown again - they were against the rules here. It would be street clothes and pajamas from now on. A return, bit by bit, to a normal life. She would be taking showers, putting on makeup, getting dressed and living by a daily schedule every day while she was there. There would be six therapy sessions every weekday and three on Saturdays. It reminded me of basic training. She would have little to say about her routine for a while. Bring it on, I thought.

It was nearing the end of visiting hours and soon I would have to leave. Susie was in a place completely foreign to her, every face would be of a stranger, and her mind unable to comprehend any of it. I told her again and again that I would be back the next day and if she wanted to talk to me someone would dial the phone for her. She was great. She told me not to worry and that she liked it here. There is no telling how many times I kissed her and told her I loved her. I had to convince her, I thought, that I was not abandoning her. I had to make sure she knew this was temporary and that I was not putting her in a nursing home. I was terrified that this is what she would think. As it turned out, I had nothing to worry about.

For the final time, I kissed her and told her I would see her the next day. And then she said, "You're not staying with me tonight?" Oh, dear God. Anything but that and I would've been all right. I almost slept on the floor. But I looked at her, and said, "Sweetie, I can't. They won't let us here. But I will be back in the morning, OK?" She nodded, I kissed her again, and then I walked out the door.

I went straight to the nurse's station. There were two employees behind the counter, and I said to them, "My wife is in room 210. This is her first night here. She hasn't been alone at night for a long time. Could you watch her extra close tonight?" I was nearly in tears and they knew it. There weren't many there who had spouses my age - usually sons and daughters were visiting their parents or grandparents. They told me not to worry; they would take very good care of her. "Her name is Susie," I said. They nodded in understanding.

I left the rehabilitation hospital that night with a broken heart. In my car, I sat in silence for a while and just stared at the mostly darkened building where my wife lay in a bed, alone, too confused to be scared. For now, at least. Leaving that parking lot was extremely difficult. I drove home in silence. I was in no mood for music. My thoughts whirled around my subconscious like a hurricane, making me dizzy and mostly unaware of my surroundings. I made it home without the slightest recollection of the drive. I walked into my house, knowing Susie would not be in it. When would she? I wondered. How much longer would my bed be empty? How many more nights would I have to leave her in this glorified home for the aged? It was then I made a vow to myself. I told myself that if she said Rick, I want to go home! I would put her in my car and take her. Hadn't she been through enough? What was I doing to her, leaving her alone? How much more of this could we take?

I mourned for my wife and the life we had. I went to bed but slept little.

CHAPTER FIFTEEN:

REHABILITATION

"I would like for her to eventually be well enough to be left alone," I said.

Brenda looked at me and shook her head. *"I don't believe that is a realistic goal."*

I went to work the next morning, but my mind wasn't on it. All I could think about was Susie waking up in her new, unfamiliar surroundings. It was driving me crazy. It was as if I was an overprotective parent worrying about a child's first day of school. I wanted to call every five minutes. I longed to be there in person. I had learned in orientation the night before that it would be beneficial to the patient if family members avoided being present at therapy sessions in the beginning. I had stated that I would not be there as often as I was at the first hospital. It would be a good way to pay more attention to the kids and our business. I knew early that first morning that I had spoken way too soon. I would also learn that the therapists themselves would encourage my involvement.

I was on my way the minute I could get away. I found a back way in that was much easier than the route I took the afternoon before. I parked and rushed up to the second floor and my wife. I found her in her room watching television. She was sitting in a wheelchair and dressed in shorts, a T-shirt and tennis shoes. She didn't, at least at this point, look unhappy. I was relieved.

She smiled when she saw me. "Hey, Rick. Are you eating lunch with me?" I looked at my watch and saw it was 11:00.

"I can do that. What time do you eat around here?"

"I'm not sure. I think there's a schedule somewhere that tells us all that stuff. I was just looking at it." She began to look around, but I didn't see anything that looked like a schedule. On the wall, however, was a large whiteboard where a daily timetable was written in erasable marker. She had three morning therapies, lunch, three afternoon therapies and then supper. I also noticed something that disturbed me. She was put on a soft diet only. Who decided that? I wondered. I would definitely accompany her to lunch.

I also noticed she had a new roommate. I introduced myself and learned her name was Mildred Wade. She was also in her 90's, a short, white haired lady with thick glasses and an attitude. She was wheelchair bound and was there to learn how to walk with a walker. I knew she was a character right away. She was constantly on the nurse's button, demanding medicine, aspirin or bathroom assistance. And she was always in a hurry. I remember vividly, five minutes after I had met her, she pressed the button. A nurse immediately answered, "Yes, ma'am, can I help you?"

"Yes, this is Mrs. Wade. I need a nerve pill!"

"Yes ma'am, Mrs. Wade. A nurse will be right with you."

No more than two minutes went by when she was on the button again. After the nurse answered, she repeated her demands for the nerve pill. "We know, Mrs. Wade, there's a nurse getting it now. We'll be there as soon as we can."

Again, less than two minutes later, she pushed the button again. After the nurse answered, Mrs. Wade said, "Where'd you have to get the pill, Chicago?" I laughed out loud.

Mrs. Wade was also on the phone a lot. In fact, it was her constant companion. No matter where she was in the room, two items had to be within reach - the phone and the nurse's button. But, really, what else is there for someone like Mrs. Wade? She was too hard of hearing to watch television. If it weren't for the telephone she would have led a very lonely existence. She had one daughter that we knew of, but she was unable to visit as often as I was. We ended up more or less adopting her. She corralled Lisa the first evening to dial the phone for her - she couldn't grasp the dial nine first for an out-side line. Lisa didn't mind, and in fact ended up memorizing a lot of Mrs. Wade's phone numbers of family and friends. Mrs. Wade would say, "Is my telephone operator over there?" Lisa would walk over and say, "You want to talk to Bobby?" Mrs. Wade would say, "Yeah. That'd be great." Lisa would dial the number. Eventually Mrs. Wade would understand the dial nine, but until then we dialed it for her.

I remember one night I heard her tell the nurses that her phone was broken. They said they would tell maintenance. This time no more than 30 seconds went by before she was on the nurses again. "My phone is still broken!" Again, they said they would report it to maintenance. Well, this wasn't good enough for Mrs. Wade. The phone was her lifeline, her whole world. Without that phone, it was similar to drug withdrawal from an addict. I asked her what was wrong with it. "It won't ring!" she said.

"Look," I said, "let me switch our phone with yours. We only use ours to call out anyway." You would have thought I just handed her a million dollars. She was so grateful. I could do no wrong after that moment.

Mrs. Wade used to call us the honeymooners. Whenever she saw us, she would say, "There go the honeymooners!" One reason for this is I was always there, from lunchtime on. Also, I made Susie walk everywhere we went, especially after we had been there a couple of days and she really began to get stronger. But since my arm was always around her to keep her from falling, it appeared to Mrs. Wade that I couldn't keep my hands off of her. That was also true, of course, and we sure didn't mind the nickname. It reminded us of a very happy time in our lives.

We became very attached to Mrs. Wade. I put together a walker for her - extremely simple - and the way she went on about it was almost embarrassing. "You can do just about any-thing, can't you?" I began to take her to the dining area with us. I cut her meat up and made sure she always got the orange sherbet ice cream. She seemed to eat better when I brought her food to her. I was glad to do it.

I remember well one evening she pushed the nurses button, and when the nurse answered she asked for bathroom assis-tance. The nurse promised to send someone. I looked at the clock because I had noticed that, for some reason, they seemed impatient with her that night. Five minutes later she rang the nurses again.

"What is it, Miss Wade?"

"I have to go to the bathroom!"

"Alright, Miss Wade, I'll send someone!" Again, she seemed impatient and bothered. This was strange because none of the nurses had ever been anything but nice to her and us. This was way out of character. I continued watching the clock while Mrs. Wade waited. Ten more minutes went by. Then ten more. She rang again.

"Yes, Miss Wade?" Really sounded put out again. Mrs. Wade told her she had to go bad. "Miss Wade, you're not the only patient we have. We are doing the best we can. You're just going to have to wait!" I let another ten minutes go by and then I had enough. I went to the nurse's station in person. There was a nurse behind the counter and I hoped it was the one who had been answering her calls.

"Can I help you?"

"Yes, you can," I said. "There's a 92 year old lady in room 210 who has been asking for the last 35 minutes for some help to go to the bathroom. It seems to me that if you are 92, and you ask for help, it shouldn't take 35 minutes!" Without giving her a chance to reply, I turned around and went back to the room. Less than two minutes later Mrs. Wade was in the bathroom. As I wrote before, this was not a normal situation in this hospital, and the fact that it was a weekend I'm sure made a difference. When I told the Monday morning nurse about it she launched a full investigation. Statements, paperwork, everything. Mrs. Wade's daughter happened to be in the room with her when I was giving my statement and she was furious. From that moment on Mrs. Wade was given the royal treatment. She deserved it.

Mrs. Wade left on the same day Susie did. They both cried. Mrs. Wade thanked me for everything I did for her. She was going to a skilled nursing center and we have talked with her a couple of times since our discharge. She is a sweet little lady and I wish for her healthy years with telephones that never break, and nurses who give her the attention she needs.

I went with Susie to lunch that first day. It was one of the few times I let her ride to a meal in her wheelchair. We got in line, and when we got inside the kitchen I told her what was on the menu. There were servers behind glass counters and the food was in hot trays between them and us, similar to waiting in a lunch line in high school. They asked for her name and room number, which I gave them. I told them Susie wanted the chicken. The server looked at Susie's chart and it was as if I hadn't said a word. She put some mashed potatoes and other soft foods on a plate and tried to hand it to me. I just stared at her. "Susie wants the chicken," I repeated.

The plate didn't move; I guessed she was hard of hearing. "There's no chicken on that plate," I said, a little louder.

"She's on a soft diet. She can't have the chicken."

Now remember, I wasn't happy about being there in the first place so I wasn't in the greatest of moods. I took a deep breath. "Susie can have anything she wants, and she wants the chicken!" The server looked over at another worker. She looked at me. "Who are you, sir?"

"I'm her husband."

"Give her the chicken." We got the chicken, but we hadn't sat down to eat for more than five minutes when we had company. Two caseworkers sat at our table with looks of grave concern on their faces. I smiled at them and asked if there was something I could do for them. "Mr. Jacobs," one of them said, "we're concerned that your wife may not be able to handle hard foods."

"She can eat anything she wants."

The other caseworker spoke up, looking over some kind of paperwork she had brought with her. "The information we received from the hospital led us to believe that she could have difficulty swallowing anything but soft foods. We're afraid she might choke."

"Listen," I said, "I was with her at nearly every meal. Once she passed her swallowing test there were no restrictions whatsoever on any of her meals. She ate hamburgers, chicken, pork chops - you name it. I'll accept full responsibility if it'll make you feel better, but I'm telling you, she can eat anything she wants." I had made up my mind that I was through playing a totally inactive role in Susie's recovery. I would make some decisions. I was intelligent enough to have some say in what would happen for the duration of her stay here. This was a good start. They seemed reluctant, but they capitulated.

"Very well, Mr. Jacobs, we'll take her off the restricted diet list."

"Thank you," I said, "and would you also look into getting the peg tube removed?" They assured me they would, but informed me that I would need to keep up with Susie's caloric intake. So, every meal from then on I listed what she ate and how much she ate. Believe me, there was never a problem with Susie's calorie count. One of our favorite pastimes between therapies was heading to the ground floor and the concession area. Susie became hooked on Payday candy bars and Dr. Peppers. And it never spoiled her appetite for dinner. She always ate well as the food was really good. It was usually hot, plenty of it and a good variety.

I got to know the servers pretty well after a while. They all wore nametags and I would address them as Miss Faye or Miss Connie. I would smile and say ma'am and tell them what a great job they were doing. It paid off.

There was always a long line of wheelchairs waiting for the kitchen to open by the time Susie and I would get there. Since Susie always walked, I would seat her at a table and wait with her until the door opened. I waited until the line was down to two or three patients to get Susie's food. It was by accident that I discovered a faster way. The door on the other side, where patients would exit the kitchen to go out to the tables to eat, was always open. I stuck my head in one evening about five minutes before the evening meal was to start, and I said, "Hey, Miss Connie, what's on the menu today?"

"Well, hey, Mr. Jacobs," she said, "we got baked chicken. Your wife loves that, don't she?"

"Yes, she does. Uh, I couldn't get her plate now, could I?"

"Sure, you can! Come on down here." And so I did. And from then on I was able to go in the back way. These servers were good people doing a tough job, and most of the patients there were very old, hard of hearing and usually in a bad mood. The employees appreciated the way I treated them and spoke to them. And I definitely appreciated the privileges I got in return.

One of our favorite places was outside in the courtyard. Just beyond the front entrance, it was a beautiful enclosed park-like area with lots of concrete benches, greenery and walking paths. There was a portable basketball goal for kids, a couple of grills and even some steps and ramps so Susie could practice her walking. It was peaceful and serene, and we spent many hours there. We talked about anything and everything. The kids could play and get noisy, and it was wonderful. One time when Scotty was playing, Susie noticed he was climbing on some handrails on one of the walks. She suddenly said, "Scotty! Get down from there before you get hurt!" Scotty was in no danger, but it was amazing to hear her say it. It was the first time she had shown real motherly instinct since she had been ill. She was really on her way to recovery.

Susie had three morning and three afternoon therapies every day she was there. Her occupational therapist, Caroline, took her through the every day tasks of living. She taught

Susie how to bathe, dress herself, put on makeup, brush her hair and teeth and everything to help make her self-sufficient and give her confidence.

Timeki was her physical therapist. She exercised her legs, taught her to walk again, how to bend down and pick things up without holding on to anything - basically to become mobile and free of wheelchairs and walkers. Susie progressed faster here than anyone dreamed she would. I feel part of this progress was due to the vast amount of time I spent walking with her during the day.

Angela was Susie's speech therapist. She would try to help Susie's mind. I went to the first couple of sessions with her, then I stopped. It was mutually beneficial for both of us that I wait in Susie's room during this hour. For Susie, because I was a distraction. For me, because it was during these sessions that I discovered just how damaged her mind was. She was unable to answer even the simplest questions: What year is it? What month are we in? Where are you? Why are you in the hospital? How long have you been in the hospital? How old are you? How many kids do you have? It was from these meetings that I saw just how far we had to go. In addition to her inability to answer these questions, she was delusional from time to time. She would call Mrs. Wade Grandma or Aunt Dink, an aunt with whom we had spent a lot of time with but who had been dead for several years. Yet, this lady was Aunt Dink. I would tell her that Aunt Dink was dead. Susie would look confused and then say, "No, Rick, that's Aunt Dink!" I would ask Mrs. Wade to tell Susie what her name was. When she did, Susie would say, "She sure looks like Aunt Dink," and be OK with it. Until the next time we would walk in the room. Again, "Hey, Aunt Dink!" and we would start the whole thing over.

Another area where Susie was delusional was watching television. There were times when she could not differentiate between what was on TV and her physical surroundings. We were watching one of the playoff baseball games when she suddenly said, "Rick, why isn't your uniform on? It's almost your turn to bat." She was dead serious.

She had one delusion that started in a hospital emergency room. Susie was sent there to have her lip looked at. This particular day, very shortly after her arrival, I arrived at the dining area to eat lunch with her. She was just coming out of the kitchen when I got there, and I noticed she was crying. I then noticed she had a busted lip. She had figured out how to unstrap herself from her wheelchair and had stood up without supervision. She was still unstable on her feet, and fell and hit her lip on a countertop in her room. They thought she might need stitches. We finished lunch and I went with her to the hospital.

We were in one of the observation rooms waiting for a doctor to take a look, and her favorite soap opera was on television. One of the main characters was having a baby. She made the comment, "Oh, Rick, look, Janie is having her baby finally." I pretended to be interested and then forgot about it. But Susie didn't. From that moment on, we had a newborn baby. As we were leaving the ER, she said in a panic, "Oh, Rick, we left the diaper bag!" I asked her what she was talking about. She said, "We left the diaper bag. We need it for our new baby!" She saw it on television, and then it became real.

This delusion remained with her for a long, long time. It became the reason she was in the hospital. For a while she didn't believe she had a heart attack, even though, prior to this episode in the ER, she would believe us when we would tell her. She was unwavering in her belief that we were proud parents of a new baby.

After the busted lip, the nurses made sure she would not accidentally get up from her chair unsupervised again. They would strap her in with knots that would challenge a seasoned boy scout. The problem with the harness is that it looked like a diaper, and I couldn't stand to see her with it on. There was one incident involving this harness that led me to never allow it on her again.

It was the first time I had been held up and I was late getting there to eat with her. It was 10 or 15 minutes past the beginning of lunch and I dropped by her room first just in case she was still there. She was, and it bothered me that a nurse had failed to check to see if she needed help getting to lunch. This was still very early on in her stay, only the third or fourth day. But what really got to me was Susie herself. She was in tears and extremely upset. They had strapped her in her wheelchair and she had been unable to get out. She needed to go to the bathroom and couldn't. She had been too embarrassed, or had been unable, to call for help. So she was wet, humiliated and all alone. I was incensed at myself for getting there late. I helped her, changed her and swore to her it would never happen again. From then on, I made sure that, if I couldn't get there, somebody would be.

I was never given a target discharge after the first day and the initial evaluation. The orientation facilitator had been wrong. Her case manager, Brenda, informed me that it would take a week or two before a target discharge with any credibility could be estimated. That was hard to take. Even though I had begun to feel better about where she now lived, I wanted her home, and I wanted to know when she might be home. I had lived under a cloud of not knowing long enough. I wanted some answers. I told Brenda this and she told me she would see what she could find out.

I saw her the next afternoon in the courtyard. She was with another case manager. I asked her if she could tell me anything at all. "Rick," she said, "I'm sorry, but there is just no way of knowing right now. We need a few days of therapy before we can set a target date."

I was upset. I asked her, "Can you at least tell me some idea of what we're looking at here? A month? Two months? More?"

"Rick, what are your goals for Susie? What do you hope we can accomplish here?"

I hadn't really thought about that. I gave her an answer that I thought would be a minimum goal. "I would like for her to eventually be well enough to be left alone."

Brenda looked at me and shook her head. "I don't believe that is a realistic goal." The other case manager shook her head as well.

So there it was. Another rug yanked out from underneath me. I heard what she said, but it was as if I had been watching as a third party. This wasn't happening. Susie will never be able to be left alone? Never drive again, either? I walked away without a word. I don't remember if I actually believed it at the time or not. Perhaps, I thought, they would always give family the worst-case scenario, and then if something better happened who could be mad? As more time passed, however, I began to believe them.

More evidence of this occurred after a week of rehabilitation. A psychologist came to her room one night, long after supper, and took her for an evaluation. I went with them, but only after promising to be absolutely quiet. He gave her a battery of tests, all designed to rate her mental awareness and alertness. As more and more of the tests were administered, I slowly began to lose hope. Her short-term memory was zero. Simple tasks were difficult. Mediocre tasks were impossible. It became clear to me, and to him, that there was extensive brain damage. After I took her back to her room, I returned to his office. I sat down and asked him, "So, Doc, what do you think?"

He took off his glasses, and then leaned back in his chair. He said, "I think that there is some damage, affecting short term memory, motor skills and her ability sort and reason."

I considered that. "So," I said, "what are the chances she'll get at least part of this back?"

He shook his head. "Very little. It's probably permanent."

"I've been told by people here that she'll likely never be able to be left alone. Do you agree with that?"

"I do."

"Well," I said, "I guess that means I'll be taking care of her from now on then, doesn't it?"

What he said next surprised me a little. "You know, Mr. Jacobs, far and away the vast majority of marriages fail after a brain injury of this magnitude."

I didn't hesitate. "Ours won't. Look, Doc, she's given me twenty years of her life, twenty of the best years a man could want. Do you think I would walk out on her now? This isn't her fault. She didn't hit her head on her boyfriend's dash during an affair. She had a heart attack. I'm not going to let her down."

He nodded. "You know, Mr. Jacobs, I believe you."

"Put it in the bank, Doc. We'll defy those odds." I got up, shook his hand, and started to leave.

"Mr. Jacobs," he said. I turned around, "You know that one exercise she was doing that she didn't want to stop?" I nodded. She was trying to connect numbers and letters, alternating from "A" to "1" then "B" to "2" and so on. She couldn't get past 3 or 4; it was just too complex for her. After five or six long minutes, the doctor tried to end her misery and allow her to stop. She moved the paper out of his reach, however, and continued on for several more minutes before she finally quit. He said, "I've been administering that test for many years. Until Susie, no one has ever wanted to continue. *Not one patient!* That, in my opinion, is significant. Build on that." I told him I would, then left his office.

Walking back to Susie's room, I wondered how much more

I could take. We had come to this rehabilitation hospital, I thought, to finish recovering. Completely. Now I had been told that complete recovery was in all likelihood impossible. While the physical and occupational therapies were going well, the mental capabilities which Susie still had were limited and would prohibit her from ever leading a normal life again.

I walked the halls of the hospital alone with my thoughts that evening. I tried to force myself to hope that this doctor was wrong, as so many others had been. What I witnessed in his office, however, was difficult to ignore. Susie was undeniably hurt, but the bruises didn't show, and it was unlikely that she would heal. At least, not completely.

"Please God," I prayed, "one more miracle."

CHAPTER SIXTEEN:

HOMECOMING

Six weeks and one day after her heart attack, I went to work knowing I would be picking Susie up from the rehab hospital and would bring her home to stay.

My God in Heaven, I felt good!

Family meetings were held every Tuesday. The meetings may be attended by any family member, and it is where information about the patient is given and questions are answered by the therapists and caseworkers. I looked forward to them with relish.

The first of these meetings went as I expected. All three therapists gave their reports. Susie was doing well, although she had a very long way to go. They wanted to keep her another three weeks, but the insurance company was balking. They would let me know. Were there any questions? I raised my hand.

"I want to take her to church Sunday. Any problems with that?"

"I don't know about that, Mr. Jacobs," Brenda said, "I'll ask Dr. Cunningham."

"OK," I said, "I'll put it another way. I'm *taking* her to church Sunday. Has anyone ever put it to you that way?"

Brenda became very serious. "Mr. Jacobs, if you take her off premises without her doctor's permission, and you get caught, then we make a report, the insurance cancels, nothing gets paid and we have to discharge her before she is ready. Please don't do it."

I was devastated. "But it's for one morning. One lousy morning. Please see what you can do." She promised, and the meeting was over.

We got the permission. I wrote a journal entry about the first time we left the hospital together:

October 14, 2001

The first time I was allowed to take Susie out of the hospital should have given me an inkling of what was to come once she was home to stay. There were so many huge advances physically; I either ignored the neurological weaknesses, or merely figured it to be a matter of time before this would improve as well. I knew of her total lack of short-term memory. This could possibly be relearned, so I wasn't too concerned. I was so happy that her long-term memory was intact that I felt I could handle anything else. As long as she knew the kids, and me, I could deal with the rest.

Or, so I thought.

I picked her up very early that morning. I was so excited to be taking her out of there that I couldn't sleep. Also, I wanted to get her ready for church at home. Get her in her own shower; not the handicapped, old people shower at the rehab hospital. But she wasn't ready to get up. It wasn't like she couldn't sleep knowing she was going to church with her family. She had no idea. Zero short-term memory.

It was devastating. One of the most pleasurable parts of a relationship is the memories. It is so much fun remembering the good times, the trips you took together, or to laugh again over a funny or silly thing that happened in the past. These things we so took for granted. What if they were gone forever? The hardest part of all this, as it has been all along, is the fear of the unknown. The fear of what the future may bring. The fear that the ache I've had in my stomach may be permanent. I'm not sure if I can live this way indefinitely.

The drive home was uneventful. I discovered her sense of direction was reversed. We were in big trouble here. She was always the navigator in our marriage. If neither of us can find our way around, there's no telling where we may end up.

The real difficulty started once we got home. I had no idea that getting ready would take so long. Her previous pet peeve of never being late was gone forever. What once took her fifteen minutes now took an hour, her movements slow and unsure. Putting on makeup and curling her hair was a marathon of time. Just walking from one room to the next test-ed my patience. Susie couldn't pass a shelf or bookcase with-out moving things around.

The key word here is patience. I had to keep reminding myself that this wasn't her fault. But I wonder, sometimes, how long can I wait before she improves? What if she doesn't get better? Will I be able to take care of her if she remains the same as she is now? Time will tell.

We were a couple of minutes late for church, but it hadn't started yet, so we were OK. This part of our day went really well. As soon as the music started Susie began to cry - and so did everyone else. It was such a thrill to be at church with our entire family taking up half a pew again. The six of us held hands during the Lord's Prayer. We had been twice without Susie when she had been in the hospital, and it had been mis-erable. I told my sister that you could take the worst time I had ever had at church - I hated going when I was a kid - and this time would have been the opposite. I was elated to be there. It was absolutely euphoric.

After church we had coffee and donuts as we always did. We went home to rest afterward. Lisa picked up some chicken after she got the boys from Sunday School. Some of Susie's family joined us for lunch, and it was thrilling having Susie home.

I had to take her back to the hospital soon after lunch. It was one of the hardest things I ever had to do. I knew then that the next time I took her out of the hospital it would be to stay. No more passes. When I told her it was time to leave, she couldn't believe it. She thought she was home for good. I hated doing that to her.

When we walked up the steps to the hospital, she suddenly turned to me and said, "Rick, aren't we going to church today?" I reminded her that we had already been. She remembered none of it.

It was one of the best mornings of my life, and she could-n't remember it. It was so very sad, like a lot of things these days. I am told that I have so much to be thankful for, and this is true. It is still very difficult, however, to be happy. I am thrilled that she is alive and should be improving physically until she is near 100%. But I am with her all the time. I see things that others don't. If things stay this way, it will be devastating.

Please God, I have asked for so much, and You have been so generous.

Please, touch her mind.

It was a day filled with mixed emotions. I really didn't know what exactly I expected. I imagined part of me hoped it would be as it always was. Perhaps I expected a magical transformation; Susie would suddenly be normal. I had only to get her out of the hospital and into familiar surroundings. Clearly this didn't happen. It was heart wrenching, but I remained hopeful that this was temporary.

Susie continued to improve physically, and I began to hear rumors of her impending discharge. The day before the second family meeting, I asked Brenda about Susie being home for her birthday on Halloween.

"Rick," she said, "I don't think she'll be here next week, much less at the end of this month!"

She explained that our insurance company was pushing for her discharge early due to her remarkable physical improvement. The rest of Susie's rehabilitation could be done on an outpatient basis, in their opinion, considerably cheaper on them.

I was thrilled. I had long thought that I could successfully take over Susie's therapy, but I remained cautious. Until I knew for sure, I would not get my hopes up. Also, Susie was certainly benefiting from her sessions here. But I ached to have her home with our children and me. I would have her packed and on our way in ten minutes should I get the word.

The word came during the second meeting. Susie would be going home Thursday, only two days away. Going home for good. On Thursday, October 18, I would wake up in bed alone for the last time. Six weeks and one day after her heart attack, I would pick Susie up from the rehab hospital and would bring her home to stay. It seemed surreal. It couldn't be really happening, could it? What a six weeks it had been. From the ambulance ride, to the ER, to CVICU, to the Acute Care and finally to rehab, it was at long last over! It was comparable to a six-year-old and Christmas. All the waiting, the interminable waiting, was finally over and Christmas morning had at last arrived. My God in Heaven, I felt good!

The afternoon before her discharge, I went and saw Brenda. I thanked her for everything she and the hospital had done for Susie. We embraced, and I turned to leave her office when she stopped me.

"Rick," she said, "hold on a second. I've got to say this. In all my years of doing this, I don't believe I've ever witnessed such devotion to anyone as you have for Susie. It is genuinely heartwarming."

"Thank-you, Brenda," I said, "I needed that. It's a labor of love, you know. I tell you, though; I can't get used to people telling me this, like it's unusual or something. What else could I do?"

She shook her head. "People just... walk away sometimes."

How sad, I thought. I tried to imagine it. I had the additional responsibility of our kids, true enough, but still, walk away? How would I live with myself? It would be as if I walked away from me. Susie was as much a part of me as I am. In other words, it simply could not happen. Not in a million years. No awards, no special accolades required or deserved. It did not take a special effort on my part to stay by her side when she needed it most. If you are driving down a road and you have a flat, what do you do? If you want to keep going, you fix the tire. It may be simplistic, but that's exactly the point. You don't abandon the car. There's too many miles left in her. If she limps a little, so be it. If she's a little hard to start, it the upholstery's a little worn, well, hey! That's life. I don't want a new car. I want Susie.

The kids and I removed most of her belongings the evening before. We told Susie we were taking her home the next morning, but it became obvious she wasn't getting it. She would ask, again and again, why we were taking her clothes out of the drawers and closet. It was unsettling, but it was far and away offset by the joy of the occasion.

I put Susie to bed for the last time in the hospital that evening, giddy with the knowledge that she would again lay beside me in our own bed the next night. I kissed her and held her for a long time in silence, wondering how it would feel to have her home after so much time of being alone. I rose up and looked at her. "Don't forget," I said, "I'll be here early in the morning to take you home."

She looked confused. "You're taking me home tomorrow?"

I told her I was. "Isn't that wonderful?"

She looked confused. "But I haven't packed anything." She started to get out of bed. "I need to pack."

I put my hand on her shoulders. "It's OK sweetie," I said, "I've already packed for you."

"You have? Are you sure?"

I nodded. "All that's left is clothes for tomorrow. Everything else has already been taken home."

She settled back down and smiled. "I'm going home

tomorrow? Really?"

"Really!" I said.

"And I don't have to come back?"

"Sweetie, you never have to come back, except maybe for an hour at a time. But, I won't leave you here alone ever again after tonight."

She nodded, smiled, and lay back down. I kissed her again, and then left her.

I returned early the next morning and got her showered and dressed. We went and saw all of her therapists, and the tears flowed. We received instructions, prescriptions and last minute farewells. Then, at long last, we walked out of her room for the last time.

With my heart nearly bursting out of my chest, and with a smile almost breaking my face in two, we walked down the hall arm-in-arm. Susie repeatedly dabbed her tear filled eyes with a tissue, and it took a great deal of self-control to keep from crying myself. All of the nurses on our floor stopped what they were doing and wished us well, and we promised to stay in touch. We reached the elevator, stepped inside, and rode it down.

I helped Susie in our car, and then we drove away. We closed the final chapter of this part of our lives, and opened a new one. Different challenges awaited us; in many ways our ordeal had really just begun. Without knowing it at the time, our lives were on the verge of becoming irrevocably changed, even more than they already had been.

Impossible? Not at all! Hadn't Susie shown us that nothing was impossible? She was a miracle, orchestrated by God, brought back from the edge of death through the power of prayer. The voices of thousands, some of whom we knew, but most from strangers, echoed in choruses up to heaven, and God, in His mercy, answered them. He was satisfied, for now, with the number of angels in Heaven. He left one on earth.

I held Susie's hand as I drove, inconceivably happy, ever-lastingly grateful. And I held new found knowledge that I would remember forever:

Life is fragile. Time is precious.

A lifetime is a gift from God.

LIFE AT HOME:

THE JOURNAL

She looked at me and said, "Well, this won't let you off the hook. I still want a really nice gift from you."

I said, "Sure. What would you like more than anything?" What she said nearly broke my heart.

"I want to get better!"

FROM THE AUTHOR

The following pages contain a journal, a diary if you will, on what it was like in the months after Susie first came home.

I was under the impression that, once she was back in our lives and in familiar surroundings, things would return to normal. I couldn't have been more wrong.

As you read, you will observe the emotional roller-coaster that I continued to ride long after she returned home. As Susie, I had good and bad days. There were literally times when I felt things were going to be fine and that I could handle it, only to find myself in total despair mere hours later. It was only through an astronomical effort, combined with huge family support and prayer, that I was able to, at last, find peace.

I did very little editing on these journals. I often repeated and contradicted myself, but I left it alone. I wanted to impress upon the reader the mayhem I experienced from day to day, and the colossal burden that I had to learn to carry and successfully deal with. These journals bear witness to the confusion, anxiety and isolation I felt every minute of every day. These were not written from memory the way the beginning of the book was. Every one was written in real time.

Writing these journals helped me cope with the overwhelming fear of the unknown and the cold realization of my sad circumstances. My laptop became my best friend and my lifeline to sanity.

THE HAND OF GOD

It's early morning the air is cold
The trees are brown and bare
My house is quiet, all fast asleep
No movement anywhere
I sit alone with just my thoughts
I wonder what will be
Will the hand of God touch my wife
And bring her back to me?

I do not cry or lament about
What is or isn't fair
The blessings I have known thus far
Have been bountiful and rare
I cry for her, my love, my life
And I ask unselfishly
Will the hand of God touch my wife
And bring her back to me?

I wake each day with hope and love
For Susie, next to me
Her eyes are closed, so beautiful
I kiss her, tenderly
I whisper, "How I love you
"And I will eternally."
Will the hand of God touch my wife
And bring her back to me?

"Oh, God," I pray, "You've done so much
"You healed my darling wife
"You touched her heart, You answered prayers
"You surely saved her life
"But please, dear God, I ask of You

"Please help my family
"Please take Your hand and touch her mind
"And bring her back to me."

Rick Jacobs

October 22, 2001

The first weekend home, and I'm not sure how I feel. It is certainly better than driving to the hospital every day. And it's wonderful having Susie next to me at night once again.

When she's sleeping, she is Susie. That's really the only time. I know it's early in her recovery. I have been told it could take years before her brain is fully healed and we know how much function she'll get back. I hope I can wait that long.

We planned a trip to Horseshoe Lake, to our cabin and pier Saturday. Lisa almost couldn't get Susie up to get dressed and ready Saturday morning. She kept calling me at work to tell me she was having trouble. I would talk to Susie and tell her to get up. She would tell me she was up, and then I would hear her call Lisa a tattletale. It's like having another child sometimes.

Susie caught two fish, a catfish and a drum. The weather was glorious, and it was almost like it used to be. She still has some coordination problems, so she had trouble reeling in the fish. She also couldn't read her romance novels between fish the way she used to, but the boys and I had a ball with her there again, especially thinking at one time that she may never make it back to the pier. I doubt I would have kept the cabin had that happened.

We went to church Sunday morning and then out for a late breakfast with Chip and Beth, our best friends. Our kids and two of their kids were there - 10 people in all. It was noisy but fun. We did some physical therapy that afternoon and then went for a walk.

I talked to my mother Saturday at work and I told her how well I was doing with Susie. She and I exercised together and walked together. This would be enough, I told my mom. I thought it would be. But as the weekend drew on and we really spent time together, I discovered something. The almost intolerable loneliness that I had been experiencing while Susie was in the hospital had not magically disappeared as I had thought. Even though she is once again with me, she isn't.

Physically, Susie looks fine. In fact, she has lost weight and really looks great. But mentally, she isn't Susie. Her speech is confusing at times. She is confused a lot. She forgets what she gets up to do. Most of all, though, there is no conversation. No real conversation at all. I really miss talking to her. We would spend hours and hours together at work and seldom tire of it - the talking anyway. We could talk about anything and everything. We laughed a lot - I could always make her laugh. She still laughs, but it is very childlike. A lot of what she does is childlike.

As good as I felt about things Saturday morning, I realized Monday, having spent the weekend with her, that I was still incredibly lonely. I understand now, that at least for a long, long time, I am a baby sitter, more or less. I have to watch her every move the way I would a very young child. I have to make sure she is bathed and ready for bed at night. I have to make sure she eats and takes her medicine. I have to follow her around when she gets up to insure she won't fall or hurt herself. She can't cook or drive. She can hardly do anything she used to be able to do.

I am now the mother, father and husband. I write the kids' lunch money checks and sign papers. I make sure dinner is made and then clean up after. I help with homework and projects. I get the kids to practice and pick them up. I knew how much Susie used to do. I made sure she had the time to do it. I wonder how I will find the time to do all of this and take care of her and our business. I feel overwhelmed and scared. But most of all I feel lonely.

I miss Susie. I miss her like hell. It kills me to see her this way. The one good thing about all this is that she doesn't seem to remember the way she was. She doesn't remember how smart and unbelievably efficient she used to be. She happily goes about her day, unable to remember what happened 10 minutes ago, seeing things that aren't there. She'll ask about the new baby we don't have and then laugh when I tell her there is no baby. Every day is her birthday. Every day is Halloween.

I don't remember what a full night's sleep is like. I write this now in the middle of the night. When I wake up and think about her, sleep won't come again. At least Susie sleeps well. I watch her a lot at night. As I wrote earlier, it's the only time she is Susie.

I've been told I need professional help. I may. I've been told I need medicine for depression. I may need that as well. What I do need more than anything in this world I can't have.

I need my wife back.

October 23, 2001

We went to Susie's first outpatient therapy session the first Monday after her release from the hospital. She will only need speech therapy. Her physical status had progressed sufficiently enough where we could finish it at home. I bought a home gym years ago and it will be perfect for her. Susie wanted me to sell it countless times - I'm really glad we didn't. We should be able to build and tone her legs and upper body with it. Our last physical therapy at home I did the exercises as well. Why not? We'll get in shape together, and it makes it more fun for her. Besides, maybe she won't feel so much like a patient but more like a workout partner. She's been a patient long enough.

The speech therapy is at the same rehabilitation hospital where she spent two weeks for in-patient therapy. It was good to walk through the doors knowing she would be coming home with me after the session. We got there early so we could visit some of the therapists and patients we got to know while she was a patient herself. She cried, of course, when we visited with them. She always does when we go back to hospitals where she spent so much time. We see nurses that she can't possibly remember at the ICU unit but she cries when they hug her. She's very emotional this way. It's funny - she never, ever gets down or depressed when she is unable to do the things that were so easy and natural before her heart attack. We tell her she can't drive, for example, and it's no big deal. Yet, here's a nurse who took care of her - Niagara Falls down her face. It's better this way, obviously. She remains mercifully unaware of her limitations.

There were three people who were patients with her that we particularly wanted to see. All three had very different reasons for being there. One of my favorites was Miss Kerry. She was an absolute delight of a lady. She was at least 80 and could not have been over four and a half feet tall. She could barely reach the table from her wheelchair in the dining room but that didn't stop her from eating. If you sat across from her, all you could see was the top of her head and two hands, a fork in one and a spoon in the other, making short work of the food on her tray. She was a frail little thing. She had broken some ribs and needed rehabilitation to walk again. But her mind was as sharp as ever and she was a joy to talk to. Susie and I got to know her well while we were there and we will miss her. She told us, during a teary good-bye, that we were an inspiration for her. That meant a lot to me. I wish her nothing but the best.

The next patient that we visited was little Becky. This poor girl was only 15 years old and was fighting cancer for the second time. Chemo had robbed her of all her hair, including her eyebrows, and there was a massive scar across the top of her head where there had been surgery. She had fat little cheeks, big brown eyes and a smile that seldom left her face. The right side of her ravaged body was almost totally non-responsive and she was bound to a wheelchair. I saw her the second day Susie was at the rehab hospital, eating alone at dinner. I walked over to her and introduced myself and asked her to join Susie and me. The look in her eyes said it all - she wouldn't be alone after all. We all got to be good friends and it was really tough leaving her. She was being fitted for a new leg brace, she told us, and was getting it Friday - could we come back and see it? Try and stop us. I still cannot understand how Susie could be struck at such an early age. I understand Becky's fate even less. This brave young lady should have been spending her time worrying about boys and grades. Instead, she would have to ask me to cut up her meat and open her milk for her. I hope someone took over after we left.

Last but certainly not least was Steven. At 26, he had graduated from college with a degree in landscaping. He was sin-

gle, living in Florida and had life by the horns. *At least until he fell out of the back of a pickup truck and struck his head on the street. This had all happened five months earlier. When we arrived at the hospital he had already been there a month and was expected to stay for several more months. He was in an open-eyed coma. He could not walk, talk or focus on anything. He could be fed but had to be watched closely and constantly reminded to "Chew and swallow, Steven!" I began talking to him the second or third day we were there. I got to know him through his mother who was always with him. I would talk to him every time I saw him. I could tell he could hear me. One day I got a "Hi, Rick." It was a thrill. By the time we were discharged, I could get him to give me a thumbs up and shake my hand. I saw real progress and hoped and prayed this young man recovered.*

It was good for us to visit our new friends. We were not alone in our misery, and we certainly found that we have much to be thankful for. After we had visited everyone, I asked Susie what she wanted to do. She said, "Don't I have to go to my room now? " It was sad. She had been home for four days, and she didn't remember. I explained to her that she never had to stay there overnight again. She seemed happy.

On the way home there was little conversation. I was deep in thought. I longed to know what the families of all three of the patients I wrote about also longed to know.

Not "why?" It's difficult enough keeping my sanity without trying to figure that out. I'll know when I ask God in person.

Will Susie get better? How much better will she get? How long will it take?

October 30, 2001

*For the first time since this whole ordeal began I'm begin-
ning to feel that I just might get through this with my sanity
intact. It has little to do with Susie's progress. In fact, Susie
has actually digressed neurologically. It's a little scary - no,
it's a lot scary - but I have to cope, just as she has to cope. For
example:*

*Susie remains unable to separate completely separate sur-
roundings. Apparently there is an area of our brain that does
this for us. It is just so natural that we, obviously, don't even
think about it. The incident watching television is an example
of what I'm talking about. Susie couldn't grasp that what was
on TV wasn't in our immediate physical surroundings.*

*Another time where this was a problem for her was only a
few days ago. Some of Sean's friends were over playing basketball with him in our driveway. Susie, looking through her
vanity drawer, thought she was missing some makeup. She
called Sean into the bathroom and told him that his friends
must have taken her makeup and she wanted it back. She was
furious - Sean didn't know what to do. For Susie it was simple. Her makeup was gone, Sean's friends were over, and
therefore his friends took the makeup.*

*We ate lunch out just a couple of days ago. I showed her
the desert menu. It had a picture of delicious looking straw-
berry shortcake on it. We used to love splitting shortcake
together. She admitted it looked good. Only a minute or two
later she asked who took the bowl of strawberries off our table.
She wouldn't believe me when I told her there was never any
bowl. The picture had become real.*

*There was a time when Susie would have delusions like this
that she would believe me when I told her that there were
"stray sparks" causing them. Not any more. This bothers me
a lot. Now, even if I have two or three others back me up, she*

*insists what she thinks she saw or heard actually happened. I
don't mind the often total lack of short-term memory - I have
learned patience is the way to handle that - but the delusions
bother me. Our younger children don't know how to deal with
it. I tell them that Susie is still their mom and they must do
what she tells them. But what do they do at 6:30 am, when she
tells them to go to their bus stop, but their bus doesn't arrive
for another 90 minutes? Especially when she now doesn't
believe them when they tell her this?*

*Another area that has me concerned is her total lack of
energy and purpose. She would stay in bed all day if I'd let
her. I have to force her to get up to help Lisa get the boys off
to school. This morning I had to literally come home from
work to make her get out of bed. She'd never get dressed if
someone didn't tell her to. She won't do anything on her own
such as brush her teeth, take a shower or do the simplest
housework. She now loves to sit and stare at the television all
day, and it makes no difference to her what's on. She's happy
just to be sitting there.*

*There was a brief period of time when it seemed, finally,
that she was bothered by her limitations. Now it's rare. This
is very worrisome to me. One night recently I was preparing
dinner. It was almost ready and I called everyone to come sit
at the table. Everyone did except Susie. I asked Scotty where
his mom was. He told me she was changing. Changing? I
asked him why, and he said he had no idea. When I went to
our room to check, I found her clad in only her blouse and
socks. She had not made it to the bathroom in time. The hardest part of this to accept is that it didn't bother her.*

*I think that this incident was, without question, the most
devastating to me of anything else that had happened since
Susie came home from the hospital. Being incontinent is
nature's way of completing total humiliation. While she was
in the hospital, modesty was thrown out the window. She also*

had no control whatsoever over when she ate, bathed, took her medicine or even slept. Enduring all of this wasn't enough. She also had to suffer the embarrassment of either asking for a bedpan or a nurse to clean her up. I watched this happen to her over and over, and my heart broke into pieces for her every time. Now, at home, I thought this part of it would end. When I saw her standing there, it brought it all back. I found her some clean clothes and helped her dress so we could eat. It was all I could do not to cry for her. I wondered if we would have to take something similar to a diaper bag in the future if we went out. Lord, I hope not. It hasn't happened since and maybe it won't again. She has suffered enough. Please, God, give her this back at least.

I opened this journal on an upbeat note and that I now thought I could get through this. While there remain many obstacles, I feel optimistic for several reasons. One reason is that Susie has glimmers of short-term memory progress. Every now and then I see where she remembers things that before would have been impossible. Today was really promising. My sister Becky picked her up for lunch with the girls. She reminded Susie that she was picking her up for bunko later tonight. When my other sister, Terri, brought her back she told Susie she would see her Saturday. Oh, no you won't, Susie informed her, she would see her tonight! This was a couple of hours later. This would have been unfeasible even yesterday. Come on brain! Rewire!

Another reason for optimism is that sometimes she knows that something is wrong with her. It's extremely rare, but every once in a while. She burst into tears yesterday because she couldn't remember something she wanted to tell me. "What is WRONG with me?" she wailed. I hugged her, tried to console her, and inside I celebrated. I told her it was nothing we couldn't fix, and I prayed I was right.

I'm working every day and I'm trying to stay focused and

motivated. It's been hard to care about anything for a while. Anything but Susie, that is. Our store hasn't meant the same to me since her heart attack. I more or less have been just going through the motions. That's got to change. I really believe it will now. I am determined to keep the doors open both for Susie and the rest of our family. It's time to move on. It's time to play the cards I've been dealt. Susie has, and now I will as well.

Depression is a funny thing. It can consume you if you let it. I've always felt I was a strong person. It's time to prove that to myself. I can do this. I can defeat the demons that have tried to control me. Two months is long enough. I still have my wife - at least part of her. I still have my kids and my family. I am so very fortunate in so many ways, and that's what I must focus on. I will look to the future with both eyes open and with the same relish that I always have. It won't be easy. The road may be bumpy. But I wrote a song once that had this bridge:

> *If life throws a lemon you make lemonade.*
> *You don't stop learnin' 'cause of one bad grade.*
> *As long as you're above ground you still got it made!*
> *C'mon life's too short to have a long face.*

Life is short. Susie nearly lost hers before she turned 40. I've always heard that's when life begins.

Let life begin.

November 4, 2001

What, please God tell me, does the future have waiting for me?

I have tried to tell myself to stay optimistic. I have always been the one to look on the bright side of everything. But it is getting harder and harder.

This is good for me - writing my thoughts down. It's better than holding it in. I'm sure this is what a therapist would tell me to do. Let it out, Rick. Don't keep it inside. So this is what I do. I write whatever comes to my mind. It's one of the very few things I do that I really enjoy these days. I have so little else. I realize this is unfair to my children. I hope they can understand.

I have vast mood swings, as is obvious in my writing. One reason for this: Susie is getting worse neurologically - something I was told wouldn't happen. She would either stay the same or get better. It's not happening. This is very hard to accept. She is nearly always delusional when she talks these days. If I ask her a question, a simple question such as what do you want for lunch at this fast food restaurant, she can answer intelligently. But any conversation that she initiates usually makes no sense. Rick, she'll say, when are the kids going trick or treating? Or Rick, who's watching the baby? There are so many delusions I can't keep up with all of them. I find myself losing hope.

We went to a Wendy's after a doctor appointment yesterday. We drove to it in her Excursion. She bought this monster SUV by herself about a month before her heart attack. When we were ready to leave, she asked where her van was. I pointed to her Excursion. That wasn't her car, she insisted. She wouldn't go near it. I unlocked the doors with the remote. She still wouldn't get in. Only when I showed her my jacket hanging on the back of the seat would she believe we owned the car.

This was almost too much. I had to fight to regain control of myself before I drove us home.

I understand that on the day I married this woman I vowed, for better or for worse, to love and honor her until death do us part. I fully intend to do so, but, so help me, I never imagined a brain injury. I would rather have her leg cut off. I could deal with that. I would still have Susie. I am no longer married to the same person I have known for the last 23 years. She is a stranger. I am reduced to the roll of a babysitter. She is a 5-year-old trapped in a 40-year-old body. There is no relationship - at least not an adult one. The last 23 years of growing together, living together and becoming so close to one another that we were inseparable, is now lost. I have to force myself to forget who she was. If I remember her as Susie, the Susie I loved more than life itself, and see the way she is now, I will, without question, go out of my mind. Sometimes I wonder, when I call her name, why she answers.

I feel almost like someone who has been sentenced to life imprisonment. Does that sound cruel? Hear me out. I am trapped in a situation that I do not want to be in. It's only been two months. It has to be similar to someone who is looking at 30 or 40 years in jail. Every day is nearly intolerable. How will I ever find the strength to last another 30 or 40 years of this? It would be easier if Susie were all I had to take care of. Maybe I could do it then. But I also have our children and our business to consider. (It may be interesting to note that at first I wrote "my" children and "my" business. Freudian slip?) I'm slammed from three sides. I'm beginning to bruise easier than I used to. Thank God for Lisa, my daughter. She has been unbelievably strong. Without her, I never would have made it this far. She's only 18, but she's light years ahead of that mentally. I hope that one day she understands just how wonderful she has been for me. I pray I will be able to show her my appreciation.

I can't get used to this constant depression. I have tried to talk myself out of it. At times I am successful, but the ache in my gut never leaves for long. There is too much of Susie all around me, both at home and at work. I find that if I have even a moment of rest or spare time, I spend it reflecting on the past. I can't close my eyes at night without thinking of her. It is far worse when she is with me. How long will this pain last? How long do I mourn?

She asked me last night when she would be able to drive again. How do you answer a question like that? I told her I didn't know, really. She would have to get her sense of direction back. She would have to pose no danger to herself or others.

I couldn't tell her that her brain would have to heal, but that it probably wouldn't. And that, for some reason, she has been sentenced to the same fate as me. She is trapped as well - in a damaged mind. She doesn't deserve this. There are scum walking on this earth - miserable excuses of human beings - whose sole purpose is to bring misery to others. Why does God allow them to live in perfect health? Does He justify this by condemning them to hell after they die?

Are we living in hell now for some reason we will understand later?

Please, God, I need answers.

November 12, 2001

I learned a lesson today.

I'm not the only one who is suffering. I'm not the only one who is hurting, or scared. There are others who are frightened. There are others who are affected by this as well.

I'll explain. My and Susie's twenty-first anniversary is two days from today. I have been really down about this lately. Our anniversaries have always been special. This one would be so different. I asked Lisa to take her shopping for my present. I made sure Susie had money in her purse, and I told Lisa I needed a new razor and aftershave. Off they went to what I thought would be a good mother-daughter bonding afternoon.

That wasn't to be. Susie had a really bad day and took it out on Lisa. They went to the closest WalMart, and as soon as Susie saw the baby aisle she starting trying to buy diapers, wipes and formula for our "baby" that she is so sure we have. It was all Lisa could do to talk her out of buying these items. It was worse after that. Susie was sure Ricky needed a new bathing suit. This is November. Lisa was nearly in tears when she called me at work after they got home.

"Dad," she said, "it was awful!"

"I know, sweetie," I said, "I'm with her every day. Oh, Lisa, what are we going to do? How are we going to make it if she doesn't get better?"

"I don't know, Dad. It scares me." And she meant it. I told her it scared me, too.

Lisa is nearly 19. She's an adult and our only daughter. She's now at the age where Mom and daughter begin to get closer. They shop together. They plan the eventual wedding. They have girl talk. Lisa must feel cheated that her mom, at least if her condition doesn't improve, will never be able to do these things with her. At least not on an adult level. I feel for her. This has got to be tough on her. And yet, she has been so strong.

I came home and took Susie to lunch with me. On the way I began to quiz her. How old are you? I'm 30. 30? I ask. Are you sure? When were you born? 1961. That's right, so how old would you be? OK, I'm 40 then. She seemed listless, uninterested. I asked her where she lived. She told me she had no idea where she lived. I asked her what her address was. Again, she said she didn't know. I said, Susie, if you got lost, and someone asked where you lived, what would you tell them? She told me her address. That's right, I said. I was happy.

She suddenly, without warning, burst into tears.

I looked at her, completely confused. "What's wrong, Susie?"

"I'm lost!"

"Susie, honey, you're not lost, you're right here with me."

She was confused and inconsolable. "But I might get lost, and then what do I do?"

I tried to explain to her that it couldn't happen. That I would always be with her and keep her safe. That I would never leave her alone. She would never get lost. She accepted that. We ate lunch without any more tears.

Later that night I found her crying again. She was really sobbing. I put my arms around and held her like a young child. Again I asked what was wrong.

"I can't write on the card I got you for our anniversary what I want to say!" She was really upset.

I said, "Sweetie, just write I Love You and sign your name. That's all I want."

"But I want to write more than that! I couldn't even get you what I wanted to. I didn't have enough money!"

"Susie," I said, and held her body even closer, "You are all I want. I didn't think I would have you on our anniversary anymore. Just being alive and next to me is the greatest gift of

all. I can't ask for more than that. Can you understand that?"

She nodded, sniffed, then looked at me and said, "Well, this won't let you off the hook. I still want a really nice gift from you."

I said, "Sure. What would you like more than anything?"

What she said nearly broke my heart. "I want to get better!" And then more heart wrenching sobs.

I held her until she stopped crying. But I couldn't make it better. Lord help me, I can't make this better. Throughout our lives together, I've always been able to say or do the right thing. I was Superman. I was Santa Claus. Whenever she would cry, I would know what to do. But as helpless as I feel, if she knows how she is, if she remembers how she was - and I now believe, at last, she does - how helpless and trapped does this poor woman feel? And is this the first step towards recovery?

I must remember this: I am not alone in my misery. There are others, including Susie, who are suffering.

Perhaps, together, we will find some peace and reason.

My Susie's mind may be hurt, but she had enough left, today at least, to send me a clear, unmistakable message:

"Help me!"

November 14, 2001

I took the second of my four children to get his driver's license today.

Ricky, Jr. turned 16 two days ago. His first car, a 1991 Chrysler convertible, was in the shop and wasn't ready until this morning. His car was also Lisa's first car. Susie and I flew to Florida to get it and drove it back for her when she turned 16. It was my mom and dad's play car, still in mint condition and low mileage. It looks good today, especially since we had a new top put on it. Ricky is thrilled. Oh, to be 16 again.

Our children have all dealt with this situation in their own way. From my vantage point, it looks to me as though they have all adjusted well. Their grades have not fallen. There has been no trouble with conduct at school and no more than usual at home. They seem happy to me, especially since Mom has come home. I've been really proud of all of them.

Lisa, 18, our oldest and only daughter, has been above and beyond since day one. Right away she knew what needed to be done and was glad to do it. Until I was able to care for the younger ones, she did. She has shopped, taken care of the laundry, worked at our business, cleaned the house, watched her mom when I couldn't and anything else I have asked of her. Without her, what has been difficult would have been impossible. All of these things she has done without a whimper, including dropping out of nursing school two days after her mom's heart attack. Her dream was put on hold, and she never hesitated. She is truly an angel on earth.

Ricky, Jr. is a tougher read than Lisa. He is in his middle teens and that's difficult enough as it is. His grades are excellent and he is able to keep them up without much apparent effort. He works at our cleaners immediately after school, and then comes home with seldom any homework. He says he does it at school - I have to believe him, at least until his grades fall. He also watches our two youngest, and he was strong during the entire time Susie was in the hospital. He relearned to say "I love you" to his mom when she was in intensive care, something he has continued even after she has returned home. He is patient with her and helps her around the house. I don't tell him often enough how proud I am of him - I hope he knows it.

Sean is our 11-year-old sports nut, musician and all around all boy. He's a good kid. He would always tell me at the hospital, every morning, "Dad, today's gonna be a good day!" I learned to count on it. He makes a point to hug his mom every day when he comes home from school. He is responsible for her while Lisa gets ready for work every morning. He takes his role very seriously and makes sure nothing happens to Susie during this time. He really missed her while she recovered at the hospital. He would ask if he could come see her every day, even after we knew she would definitely come home again. They were buddies, Susie and Sean. They still are.

Scotty is six. He's our surprise baby. Obviously, since he just started kindergarten, he spent far and away more time with us than the others. We didn't tell him much while Susie was really sick. He would get on the bus every morning and ride it home every afternoon. He would ask about her, I would tell him she was still sick. He would ask when she would be home, and I would tell him pretty soon. This was good enough for him. But he began sleeping in our room a couple of weeks into her hospital stay, and since she's been home he seldom leaves her side. He'll sit by her watching TV at night and then sleeps next to her every night. I mean every night. It's as if he's afraid she'll be gone again. I haven't stopped him from doing it yet. It gives him comfort when he has had very little for a long time. I know how he feels. I sleep next to her every night as well. There was a time that I wasn't sure it would ever happen again.

Anyway, Ricky is now a licensed driver in the state of Tennessee. I tried to explain to him how wonderfully danger-ous a motor vehicle is. It is freedom in the truest sense of the word. It can also kill you. Or worse, it will cripple or maim you or someone riding with you. I warned him of the dangers of a moment's distraction. I said I remembered when I was his age. I was invincible, just as he is. Or thinks he is.

When you are 16, I said, nothing bad can happen, right?

When you are 39, you can't have a heart attack, right?

I think that stopped him, then and there, and he began to think. He just may have understood what I was trying so hard to explain. Life is uncertain. Sometimes it is horribly unfair. Sometimes the unthinkable can happen, and happen to those close to you. So close that he just might imagine it could hap-pen to him.

And really, I've seen the inside of enough hospital rooms to last for a long, long time.

So be safe, Ricky, Jr. May God watch over you wherever you may go in your newfound freedom. May your guardian angel never go on break. Keep your head clear, your eyes open and your senses sharp. Come home safely every night.

Because, you see, it's good when your entire family is all under one roof. The roof that covers the place you call home.

November 19, 2001

It's been a rough couple of days.

The medicine I was so hoping would help Susie's mind hasn't worked. At least not yet. I realize that it's only been a couple of weeks, but still, she is as confused as ever. Maybe even a little more than she was. It's too much to bear sometimes.

She tried making iced tea last night. I walked into the kitchen and there was water all over the counter. She had poured way too much water into the tea maker. What was worse, though, was that she had tried to make what holds my coffee filter fit on her tea pitcher. She even had the tea bag in it. I took over for her, of course. I felt so, so sorry for her.

She now thinks it's Thanksgiving every day. When she thought it was Halloween every day I could tell her only once that it wasn't and she would be fine. Now, however, I have to tell her every few minutes that it is not Thanksgiving. When we leave the house, she will suddenly burst into tears. I ask her what is wrong, and she says she has forgotten to make a dish of food to take to Grandma's house. I tell her, again, that Thanksgiving is not until Thursday. She has to look at a calendar before she will believe me. Then, on the way to wherever we are going, she asks where the baby is. And later, is the food in the back or did we leave it on the counter?

This is beginning to affect her as well as the rest of us. She cries a lot more now. She is so afraid I will get tired of her, or that I don't like her anymore, and that soon I will leave her, or put her in a nursing home. I have never given her a reason to suspect any of this. She is becoming more and more paranoid. I will really watch how I act around her now. She doesn't need to worry about anything except getting better.

We went to Sean's first basketball game yesterday as well as a movie for the first time. She did really well at both places. She ate a ton of buttered popcorn at the movie and two hot-

dogs at Sean's game. She knew when to cheer for our team and watched the entire movie without a problem. There are times when no one would ever know. When she went into the bathroom by herself at the theatre, though, I was worried to death. It seemed like she took forever. She came out intact, however, and I had no need to worry at all.

We got up to go to mass this morning. I got her up in plenty of time to get ready. Being on time wasn't meant to be, however. She just can't get ready on time. She has a terrible time putting on makeup. Every morning she gets furious that someone has stolen her blush, eye shadow or some other cosmetic. I have to get Lisa to help her find these things. I am helpless here. I have found that whether I give her a half hour or an hour and a half, she still won't be ready on time. We haven't made it to mass before 9:00 yet. I leave the room and let her take her time now. This way I won't lose patience. If people at church don't understand, that's tough. We're just late. I get Lisa to take the boys now, and they save us a seat.

There was a couple sitting in front of us at mass with an adorable baby boy. He was not older than four or five months. This couple got nothing out of the mass. Their entire focus was on their baby. I couldn't blame them. He smiled the whole time. He was really good. I envied them. I remember when our own kids were that age. Those were good times. Susie loved her babies. She was in her element when they were that young. She knew instinctively what to do and when to do it. I was always in awe of her. She knew when shots were due, when they were sick enough to go to the doctor or if she could doctor them herself, when it was time to eat, sleep or be changed. And she could hear the first whimper from a mile away and behind closed doors. She was the best mother a child ever had.

I long for those days again because Susie was still Susie. I look around at mass now and I see so many couples. I'm jeal-

ous of all the husbands. Their wives aren't brain damaged. They are able to keep the kids together, drive to and from church, go to work on Monday morning and prepare dinner tonight. They can talk about the kids' grades, when the open house is and do you need anything while I'm out. These couples do things together the way Susie and I used to. They can still plan for the future. They don't have to take a wait-and-see attitude about what the future will bring. Maybe she'll get better, maybe she won't. Do we still plan a 25th anniversary cruise? Do we even have a normal future, or will it be like this forever? Sometimes I feel that, if it stays this way, I will have been cheated out of some of the best years of my life.

I've noticed when Susie cries now, it doesn't affect me the way it used to. Before she got sick, it would kill me. Now, it's as if one of my very young children are crying. I'm heartbroken, and I hold her the way I would hold a toddler, assuring her that everything will be OK. I kiss her cheek, wipe her tears away and stay with her until she stops. It's funny, though, how I see her now. As a baby, or a very young child. I see the adult, ever so slowly, slipping away. Our relationship as husband and wife is dwindling. I fear, if she doesn't improve, it will be gone forever. There has been no physical relationship for a while now. It's like making love to a complete stranger. It's incredible for me to say this, but I'm just not interested.

Oh, Susie, where are you, sweetie? Are you in there somewhere, deep down, trying desperately to come to the outside? Are you longing for me the way I so desperately long for you? Are you crying out to me in a slowly softening voice? Do I hope forever, or do I prepare myself to care for you as a child for the rest of our lives?

I will do this, should that be our fate. For better or worse. Until death do us part.

I will be there to wipe away your tears every time you cry out to me.

But who, God tell me, will wipe away mine?

November 20, 2001

In two days it will be Thanksgiving.
This will be the first real holiday since Susie's heart attack.
It is also the first holiday since she has been home. Her birthday, Halloween and our anniversary don't count, because our families did not gather together the way they will on Thursday. I have mixed emotions.

I will assist Susie in making the orange Jell-O salad that has become a tradition over the years. I dearly love this desert, and I look forward to it every year. This year she will be unable to make it by herself. This seems strange.

Since it is Thanksgiving, I owe it to myself, and my family, to count our blessings and to realize that we have much to be thankful for. Here goes:

Susie is alive and well, physically. There was a time where I thought I would have to face the holiday season without her. I thank God every day that she remains with us. Thanksgiving and Christmas would be meaningless without Susie to share it with.

I have four wonderful children. All of our kids are in good health, they do well in school, they haven't gotten into any trouble and, as far as I know, do not do drugs or drink alcohol. We have a great deal to be proud of.

I have a business that allows me to spend time with Susie and the kids. I'm very fortunate here. I do not have a 9-5, punch a clock job. I leave when I want. I can take Susie to doctor appointments, therapy sessions and even out to lunch once in a while. This is indeed a blessing.

I have been blessed with an immediate family who has gone way above and beyond the call of duty. Since Susie has been home, I rarely go a night without hot food. Never a day goes by without a phone call. My sisters, Becky and Terri, keep me motivated to continue writing by boosting my ego with every chapter or journal I fax them. They also have helped keep my sanity intact by continually reminding me that they are there to help if I need it, that I need only call. I hope they realize how important this has been. They are my heroes.

I have my own health. This is important, especially now. While I wait for Susie to get better, I have to be strong for her and my kids.

God kept me strong during a time where it would have been easy to give up. I don't know how I was able to keep going at times. I had lots of help, both here and from above. There are cracks in the armor, but I remain standing and determined.

My family and I sleep under a roof that keeps the rain outside, inside walls that keep the cold wind from penetrating and under covers that make us feel safe and warm. We live in freedom. We aren't afraid to walk outside. There are no bullets flying across streets or from building to building. We live in a country where ambition is encouraged, and we can dream without limits. Susie is alive today because our hospitals are filled with the best doctors in the world. God bless America.

I am especially thankful that, for more than 20 years, I have been blessed with a love that so rarely comes along. I was fortunate to have understood this before it was too late. Susie and I found each other in a world where billions of people live. I would not have been happy with anyone else. God made Susie, and then gave his angels instructions to save her for me.

I am thankful to have known others during Susie's recovery and rehab who made me realize that we are so much better off than we could be. I wish them all well during this season.

Finally, thank you Susie. You made the choice to spend your life with me. You gave me four children. You stood behind me at every turn in our lives, both good and bad. You made the bad times tolerable. You made the good times unfor-

gettable. There has not been a time in my life that wasn't made way more special because of you. I am nothing without you, I am everything with you. I vow to stand with you through this. You will never be alone.

There, I feel better. I needed to write these things down. Sometimes, I get just a little overwhelmed, and it is easy to focus only on what I have lost, not what I have kept. It would be similar to someone who lost an arm in an accident. For a while, I'm sure, there would be agony over the loss of one limb, until, finally, he would appreciate that he still had the other three.

I don't know yet how long it will take for me to fully appreciate my other three limbs - my kids, my immediate family and my way of life. Because, right now, my right arm is barely hanging on, and the pain remains unbearable at times. Only time will tell whether or not it will heal, or fall off completely.

I will wait. I have no choice.

I pray that next year's list will be easier to write.

November 24, 2001

I've heard that time heals all wounds.

Maybe. The wounds I have suffered are pretty bad, though. I wonder how much time would have to pass before I feel some of these wounds healing? I don't believe time will be a powerful enough drug to work for me. Time won't replace Susie, or the life we had. Sorry, time, it just isn't going to happen.

So, then, what am I going to do? How about prayer? Prayer's good. Come to think of it, I believe this is what got her out of a hospital bed in the first place. In fact, I know it was. We had nearly every state in the union represented by prayer, plus some foreign countries as well. Most faiths were praying for her. It reminds me of the beginning of the movie "It's A Wonderful Life" where all of the prayers were going up to heaven at the same time. God just couldn't ignore all of that divine communication.

So I began praying for her mind's recovery. I have asked others to keep Susie's name on their prayer lists. And I think it's working.

Here is a wonderful example. We were driving home a few nights ago, when suddenly Susie said, "Oh my gosh, Rick, we forgot about the baby!

"There's no baby, Susie." This has become extremely routine. Usually that will end it. Not this time. "We have a baby, Rick! I know we do!" She was adamant. Scotty was in the back seat. I looked in the rear view and made eye contact with him. "Scotty, tell Mom who our baby is."

He said, "Mommy, I'm your baby."

Susie looked at me. "He's our baby, Rick?" I told her he was. "We don't have another baby that's a week old or so?" I told her no. "Are we on our way to Grandma's for Thanksgiving dinner right now?" I told her Thanksgiving was the next day. She became quiet.

I alternated between watching the road and her. I could tell she was upset. Sure enough, I saw the eyes water and then the tears begin. Susie's very emotional. I asked her why she was crying. "Because I don't know anything! I'm stupid!" The tears really began to flow now. I pulled over and stopped.

"Susie, you're not stupid. You had a heart attack. Your brain was injured. It's not your fault. But I'm glad it upsets you. It means you know! That's a big step."

"I know you're getting tired of me! You're not going to want me around!" Heavy sobbing now.

"Susie, don't ever think that." I looked back at Scotty. "Scotty, tell your mother something. Would you rather have a mommy on Thanksgiving that you would visit in a graveyard, or one who is with us who's a little confused sometimes?"

Scotty unbuckled his seatbelt and put his arms around Susie's neck from the backseat. "I want a mommy who is here!" I couldn't have said it better myself. Then it was my turn.

"Sweetie, I will never, ever give you a reason to think I will one day get tired of taking care of you. But I want to ask you something: Do you want to get better?" She nodded and said yes. "Then you got to do something for me. You have to try, you have to try hard. You have to get stronger, you have to help me with the kids, and you have to help around the house. Can you do that for me?" Again, she said yes. We drove home.

Thanksgiving was yesterday. She got up early and without a hassle. She put her makeup on without help and without problem. And she looked beautiful. We went to her grandmother's house for lunch and then to my mother's for supper. She mingled, ate and had fun. She helped clean up. It was wonderful. There were times when she was confused, but it didn't happen often and it wasn't serious.

The best was yet to come.

When we got home, she was exhausted. I helped her into her pajamas. We went to bed at 8:30 or so and watched a movie for a while. I turned out the lights about 9:00. That's when the miracle happened.

"Rick," she said, "wasn't today fun?"

"It really was," I said. "What was the best part for you?"

She thought. "At Grandma's house, it was seeing Uncle Jimmy." I was stunned. Her Uncle Jimmy lives in New Mexico and drove up for the holiday. It was a surprise. No one knew he would be there. And she remembered! Two days ago - maybe even one day ago - that would have been impossible. I was pumped now. I kept going.

"Where else did we go?"

"We went to your mom's house. Wasn't it good seeing Brad and Cara there?" It was good, but it was even better she remembered them. Brad is my niece's boyfriend, and Cara my nephew's girlfriend. She hasn't seen them more than a half a dozen times total in her life. This is real evidence of short-term memory. If we get that back, it will be huge.

"Susie, I am so proud of you. You remembered all of that! That's unbelievable!" She smiled at me. Then she asked, "Can I lay my head on your chest like I used to?" Like I would say no. I lifted my arm, her face raised up to mine for a kiss, and then her head was on my chest. I put my arm around her, and it was as happy as I've been in a long, long time. This is how it was for more than 20 years. She would always, at some point in the night, end up like this for a little while. And, for a little while, it was like it was.

God answered my prayers from a long time ago. Please, God, I would say, I can't face the holidays without her. He obliged. Lately I've prayed for her mind to heal. And on this Thanksgiving Day, there was unmistakable evidence that, a little at a time, He's answering this prayer as well.

I held her in my arms until we were both asleep. And for

the first time since her heart attack, I slept until my alarm woke me. She lay beside me, eyes closed, breathing easily and comfortably. I kissed her cheek. It was reminiscent of a time long ago.

Or, was it a peek at what may be again?

November 27, 2001

There is only one Susie in this world.

She has brown eyes. Her eyes look at me with love. They are always glad to see me. They find me in a crowd of people to make sure I am still there. Her eyes smile at me. They sometimes wink, especially in exchange for one of my winks, as if to say, "I love you, too." Occasionally, they cry. I'm sad when her eyes cry. Because I know they cry out of frustration. The words won't come. The memory doesn't work like it used to. Her eyes will see things that aren't there sometimes. Still, her eyes see me, and they see our children. They are the most beautiful eyes on earth.

Susie has a beautiful face. On her face are lips, delicate and lovely. They are so very kissable. I never tire of it. Her lips smile most of the time. There was a time when they didn't. I missed her smile. When she smiles at me now I feel relief, happiness and excitement. Relief, because I know she is alive. Happy, because she is happy again. And excitement, because her smile has excited me for almost a quarter of a century. Her lips are sad as well at times. They are sad because they say things that don't make much sense sometimes. Or they can't remember what to say. Still, her lips will say "I love you, Rick." That's good enough for me. They are the most beautiful lips on earth.

She has beautiful hands. They are small and delicate. Her nails are long and lovely. They always have been. Her hands fit perfectly in mine. I love to hold them. We hold hands a lot now because she has a little trouble walking and may lose her balance. I hold them gladly, not only to hold her up or to help her walk, but because it is still so very pleasurable. Her hands are at the end of her arms, and together they are again able to hug. They hug our children and me. There was a time when these arms and hands were unable to move. We did not know whether they would ever move again. They are the most beautiful hands and arms on earth.

Susie has beautiful legs. They are long and thin. She will bend them and snuggle against me at night. She walks from place to place with them. There was a time when we wondered if she would ever walk again. Her legs were weak and tired. They are getting stronger every day. I am thrilled every time we walk together. They are the most beautiful legs in the world.

She has a mind. It is a beautiful mind. Sometimes her mind will play tricks on her. I tell her when this happens. Sometimes she is aware of her new limitations and it makes her sad. Sometimes she is so sad she cries for a long time. When that happens, I am sad as well. I try to be strong for her. I tell her how far she has come, not how far she has to go. Her mind is doing better sometimes, and I have great hope. Occasionally her brain has a tough day and it's as if we take steps backwards. I refuse to lose hope again. I refuse to think negatively. Because her mind won't. It's the most beautiful mind on earth.

As time passes, I have learned to look at my wife in a new way. I read the paragraphs I have just written and they tell me something. They tell me I have much to be excited about. I have been given the privilege of taking care of this beautiful woman. No longer can I dwell on the past. I must look to the future and fulfill this obligation to the best of my ability. She will be happy because of me. She will feel safe because of me.

Watching television last night gave me the first idea of the importance of my job. There was a movie that had some violence in it. She suddenly grabbed my arm. "What's wrong?" I asked her.

"Those men scared me."

"The ones on TV?"

"Yes," she said, "the ones with the guns."

I've told her the difference between TV and real life before. Usually she gets it, occasionally she doesn't. This time I didn't try to explain it again. I put my arm around her and said, "Sweetie, no one will hurt you while I'm around. OK?" She nodded, and I felt her relax. I found a different movie.

What a thrill it was to be this important to someone. She felt safe with me. I'm nobody special, yet to Susie at that moment, I was her protector. I made her feel secure. I'm not sure if I have ever felt so good about anything in my life.

I vow to never take this roll for granted. I'm lucky to be married to this girl. It took me a long time to figure this out. Try this. Go back and re-read the first five paragraphs. Only this time, where it says 'has' substitute 'had'. Where it says 'are' substitute 'were'. Where it says 'is' substitute 'was'.

Susie may be a little different, but so am I. I'm more important to her. I make more of a difference to her. And, occasionally, I'm larger than life to her.

And that's what this is, really. A celebration of life. Susie's life.

Long live Susie. May we grow old together. May God give me the strength to never let her down. May I always understand how lucky I am to accompany her throughout the rest of her life.

I'll miss the way she was. I'll love her the way she is.

I don't have to take care of Susie.

I want to.

November 30, 2001

I saw a horrible accident on the way home today.

I didn't see it happen. I came up on it long after it had occurred. At first I was put out - traffic was held up and I was in the line of traffic. I saw the brake lights. I changed lanes and maneuvered to the fastest route to the intersection. I made the right choice. I got to the scene faster than the other lane. What I saw before they did was shocking.

There was what was left of a vehicle blocking the intersection. The front driver's wheel wasn't where it was intended to be. Amazingly, it was intact and inflated, but it was several feet behind the driver's door. Read that again - several feet behind the driver's door. I can't imagine how that happened. The front and rear wheel were nearly touching. I then beheld the most gruesome scene I may have ever laid eyes on.

The steering wheel and the front driver's seat were together. They were as one. They were meshed. There was no space whatsoever between them. Whoever was driving that vehicle was no longer a part of this world. Period. No question, whatsoever, about it.

It was a startling moment in my life. Whatever I had been through up to that point in time, it would not compare to the shock of the family who would get the call from the scene of this accident. There would be no hope that we had. There would be no "he might still be alive" whispers from family and friends. This driver was dead. The only question would be how much of the body would be remotely recognizable to loved ones. I hope memories are strong and vivid. There is no way in hell that family would get one last hug, or kiss, or tearful goodbye. This human being was, and forever would be, gone.

I stared at the car, or at least what was left of it, and tried to imagine what this family would be going through for the next day or two. Funeral homes, funeral arrangements and burials would dominate everything else for the immediate future. Nothing else mattered. Whatever had happened to that point in time, really, suddenly became totally unimportant. Arguments, debts, loans, mortgages, children, love and relationships abruptly ended. Period. Whatever thought went through the mind of the loved one at the last moment of his or her life would be completely private and secret. I love you, mom. Oh, my God. This isn't happening. Forgive me, Jesus. This can't be real.

And then, abrupt, total blackness. Or is it? No one knows, because no one has been there and then come back. There is talk of the tunnel, the bright light at the end. There is the falling, down, always toward the comforting light, no fear whatsoever. Too many people have experienced this for it to be made up. I believe it exists. I'm sure Susie saw it.

Then the weird thing happened. It would be too easy to make up for it to be made up. As God is my witness, once I passed the terrible wreck, and all of the police and ambulances and fire trucks, I saw more blue lights ahead of me. It soon became obvious what it was. It was a funeral.

A funeral. Suddenly, there was a death behind me and one in front of me. And the one in front of me was one very popular individual. There had to be fifty cars in the procession. I couldn't help but think the two deceased were talking to each other.

"Is that you in front of me?"

"Yeah."

"What happened?"

"You know, I was in a hurry. Tried to make the light."

"Didn't make it, did you?"

"No."

"You got kids?"

"Yeah."

"How many?"

"Three."

"What are they gonna do, now?"

"Don't know."

"You know, man, I was almost 80. It was my time. How old were you?"

"Twenty. Almost."

"Almost twenty? Good Lord, man, I had sixty years on you. What a waste."

"Yeah. I wish I could do it over again, know what I'm saying?"

I do. If there was a way to do it over again, the things I would do differently. The first time there was a pain, I would take her in. I would not believe the doctor when he said it was merely acid reflux. When Susie said it was hurting more than it should, I would believe her. If I had to carry her to the hospital in my arms, I would. Give me the chance, God, to do it over. The same chance that the driver of that mangled car would love to have. To approach that intersection again, and instead of flooring it, just maybe applying the brakes. Then, making it home. Kissing his kids. No funerals. No wakes. No pain. No anguish. No crying.

Life would go on. And wouldn't that be nice?

Slow down. Don't beg for a second chance that isn't there.

The pain is beyond anything you can imagine.

December 3, 2001

OK, there are advantages to all of this.

I have been the benefactor of a multitude of silver linings. Because of Susie's new limitations, I have to be with her many hours a day. We used to spend a lot of time together, but nearly all of it at work.

What we do together now differs dramatically from our old life. I still work in the mornings, but then I come home and we eat lunch together every day. A leisurely lunch, not an inhaled one so we can get back to work. We take as much time as we want. I then try to get her to walk with me for a half hour or so. I'm not always successful - sometimes she just feels too tired. If there are no doctor appointments or therapy sessions, I'll let her nap on those days, getting some solid writing in before the kids get home.

I have a couple of hours with the two younger boys between school and supper. We get homework done; we watch television. They make it a point to hug their mom every afternoon. It's been a long time since we were home when they got home. They no longer have to go straight to the cleaners after school. They enjoy their time at home with us. Susie and I enjoy it, too.

We eat supper every night together. We used to do this, but at a restaurant, and usually no earlier than 8:00. Now it's at home, and we try to eat about 6:00 so we can watch "King of the Hill." Susie especially enjoys this show. Before she was sick, she would never watch anything but the news or weather. She laughs at silly things now, and this cartoon is nothing but silly. Susie loves to watch this show, so we watch it.

We then spend the rest of the evening together. I'll quiz her on her memory, get her to write in her journal or do some flash cards. A lot of times she and Scotty play together. At times they can go for thirty solid minutes and do nothing but laugh. I wonder if Susie's brain is at Scotty's level of maturity. Obviously she is able to read and write far above the ability of a six-year-old, but when I watch them, well, occasionally it appears they are like playmates. Good enough. She's here to play, and I'm grateful.

Weekends are the best. We have started going to the movies on Saturday afternoons. We take the two youngest boys with us, pick out a movie, get lots of buttered popcorn and watch a movie together. We never, ever used to be able to do this. It seems like I remember that this is what families do together. I know we see lots of families doing this very thing every Saturday with us. The last two Saturdays, Sean had a basketball game after the movies. We all went and watched him play, and lo and behold, his team won both games.

On Sundays we go to church. I'm not sure what Susie gets out of it any more. How she used to love being at church as a family. It's the one thing we still make Lisa do with us. We always get donuts after, and then usually brunch somewhere. The rest of Sunday I leave up to Susie. Sometimes we walk. Sometimes we watch football or golf. Since her heart attack, she loves sports on TV. Go figure.

Quality family time has resulted from this horrible event in our lives. God doesn't cause or plan heart attacks, but once He hears our prayers He will help us through them. He will enrich our lives in other ways. I would not have chosen to change our life from the way it was prior to September fifth, but I am grateful that God made Susie better and then allowed us to reap some benefit from this tragedy.

Oh, and there are other advantages that I wouldn't have thought of. Of course, I'm not 16, and the situation would not have presented itself to me. But my son, Ricky, is 16, and, the situation did present itself to him. I'll explain.

Ricky had an interim report card that needed to be signed. In geometry, he had a 78.5%. He knew that I would not be the least bit happy with this. Well, he figured, a parent had to sign this interim. And, of course, Susie is his mom and, therefore, a parent. Never mind she wouldn't have any idea of what she would be signing. I'm sure the conversation went like this:

Ricky: "Mom, I need you to sign this."

Susie: "OK."

And then it was signed. And he would've gotten away with it had his geometry teacher not called me. You see, Susie's signature is still not real stable. It looks like a little girl's handwriting. His teacher was making sure it wasn't a forgery. Nice try, Ricky. Man, he is way too much like I was at 16.

Which is why I didn't get too mad at him. Technically, he did nothing wrong. A parent had to sign, a parent did sign. For this to work, though, the parent would need to know what she was signing. I set him straight. Don't let this happen again! Yes, sir. You knew exactly what you were doing, didn't you? Yes, sir. Why did you get her to sign it, anyway? Because you were at work, and she was at home.

And she was at home. Five of the sweetest words my son has ever said.

Who could stay mad?

December 9, 2001

They especially love the night.

I'm talking about the demons. Those miserable, stubborn creatures that haunt me relentlessly, but more so when I am trying to get some desperately needed sleep. And since they know I have managed to get beyond my fear of them, they are now satisfied to endlessly taunt and tease.

They normally let me sleep until about midnight. From then, until I finally surrender and get up, they talk to me. Not out loud, of course. Oh, no. They make sure that I am the only one who hears them. This way, the loneliness that I am occasionally overwhelmed with is intensified, a constant reminder of what may be for many years. Or maybe forever. The whispering voices invade my subconscious, as maddeningly as a dripping faucet, making sound sleep a long lost memory:

"Susie's not the same, Rick!"

"You're all alone!"

"Forget all the plans you had!"

"You'll never pay all the bills coming in!"

"Your business is in trouble!"

"What are you made of, Rick? Can you do it? Can you? What will happen in the next five years? Can you wait that long?"

I close my eyes. I try like hell to go back to sleep, hoping they will go away. They'll normally allow me to get to the verge of blissful void, only teasing me into believing they had left. Then the daggers of their truths all come at once, slamming into my brain, until I sit up, sweating, and give in to their cruelty. I look over at my wife, sleeping, happily unaware of the burden I carry. I get out of bed to face another day of uncertainty and the never-ending barrage of demons.

Understand that last line: The never-ending barrage of demons. It's so very true. Every minute of every day I live with the nightmare of my world having been turned upside down. It doesn't matter where I am or what I'm doing; it never, ever goes away. It makes no difference whether Susie is with me or not. The demons remain with me, making sure I'm never allowed a moment of peace, insuring that the memory of the way Susie was stays beside the reality of the way she is, occasionally driving me to the edge of insanity. I couldn't prepare myself for this - the 24-hour-a-day onslaught. They're there, though, always with me.

I feel I have managed my new life pretty well to this point. I have learned to take care of Susie. I have attempted to balance my wife, kids and business, neither neglecting nor spending too much time with any one of them. There are times when I relish my new role in life as Susie's caretaker. There are also times when I so desperately miss my wife and the days when she was my partner, my lover and my companion. She was every bit my equal, so gifted and so loving. I am torn between remembering the past and trying to forget, to start a new life with this woman I call Susie.

I feel as if I'm continually searching for something. I don't know what it is, though. I know it's not sympathy - there are those a lot worse off than me. I go through each day with a sense of never ending questions going through my mind. Why did it happen? Why did it happen to us? There must be a reason, a purpose of some sort. Will I understand before it engulfs me? Will I let these demons have the satisfaction of defeating me?

I have written many times about the continual roller coaster that I have been on these past few months. My life has been a series of ups and downs. I'm tired of the ride now. I want to get off. It's like a twilight zone. I come to the end of the ride, but I see the operator shaking his head and laughing as I go by, over and over. I can't jump out because I can't leave Susie by herself. She's more scared than I am. I have to *remember that.*

So, I live with the demons. I hear them laughing at me, daring me to get back up after they knock me down. It's almost like Rocky Balboa. I hear voices telling me to stay down. But what happens then? Leave Susie by herself? Not a chance in hell. The same hell these demons come from.

I have the same advantage that Rocky had during his fight. I have a cheering section. I have family and friends at ringside helping me, encouraging me and giving me strength. I have faith in God. And I have faith in Susie, the Susie I used to know, the Susie that I have to believe is still in there somewhere, fighting demons of her own. She is going through the same struggle I am, desperately trying to get off the mat, trying to beat the terrible odds stacked against her.

I know she's doing just that. Because at night, especially at night, she'll ask me to hold her. She'll cling to me for hours, resting comfortably, knowing the demons cannot get to her as long as I am there.

Rest, Susie. Be at peace. I will be there for you. I will always be there for you.

The same as it ever was.

The same as it ever was.

December 12, 2001

We were walking hand in hand, my little girl and I. It was a beautiful afternoon, unseasonably warm for this time of year. The sun shown down bright and warm, a gentle breeze blew another leaf off a tree now and then, and it was reminiscent of a glorious spring day. It was difficult to imagine that winter was very nearly upon us.

We decided to take advantage of the reprieve that Mother Nature had granted us and began a second trip around the block. I imagined that my little girl's legs would be very tired before we finished - she had never tried twice around before - but she gallantly accepted the challenge. "If I get tired, you can carry me," she teased.

As all very young minds will do, the walk became a game. I noticed she was taking great care not to step on the sidewalk cracks. I asked her about it. "Step on a crack, break your momma's back," she responded. She noticed I wasn't playing. "Your momma's back is really gonna be broke!" she cackled, continuing to play on her own.

She was so cute. Sometimes her steps had to be very long in order to avoid the cracks, and other times very short. There were occasions where the sidewalk was full of cracks, probably from some very cold winter weather, and she would drift onto the adjacent grass so her momma could stay healthy. Her determination was clear. I don't believe her foot even once came near a crack.

We were about halfway through our second time around when she began counting. She counted every single crack on the sidewalk, one at a time. Through the 20s, 30s, 40s, and on and on. When she got to 100, I thought she would tire of this new game but such was not the case. She continued the counting. All the way to our front door, 240 cracks. She was exhausted but happy. I found a pillow for her and put her on the couch to rest. She curled up underneath an afghan her grandmother had made for her years ago and soon fell asleep. I kissed her cheek, and then went to my kitchen to write.

I stared at my computer for a long time, my mind blank. My eyes would stray to the counter top where my little girl's purse rested. Inside this purse was a driver's license that said she was 40 years old. A driver's license that identified her as Susan Jacobs.

Both are lies, really. She may have been born 40 years ago, but she isn't anywhere near 40. Oh, she wants to be, in fact she tries very hard to be sometimes. But the vast majority of the time she remains, sadly, a little girl. A young child who needs constant supervision, companionship and love.

The other lie is her name, Susan Jacobs. I remember Susan Jacobs. She was a beautiful, smart and incredibly loving person, a wonderful wife and mother. She could cook, clean, take care of our kids and do all of this around a 10-hour workday at our business. She remembered dates and times, had a marvelous sense of direction and loved her husband the way he loved her - with everything she had. The little girl on the couch was not Susan Jacobs. She may resemble her, and there are rare times when, for a moment, for a brief, wonderful moment, a tiny little bit of my Susan surfaces. But she is usually gone before I really realize she was ever there.

Also inside her purse is a broken wedding ring. My broken wedding ring. The band has gotten thin over the years and it breaks. It looks as if there is a piece missing.

That's sort of prophetic, don't you think? There is a gap in my ring that prevents it from being whole. The gap isn't large, and yet, the two ends will never touch without the missing piece.

Sort of like Susie and I. There's a piece missing, and I wonder if we will ever find it. We, like the ring, will never be the same without it.

The ring can stay in her purse for now. It was representative of a happier time. For now, I'll take care of my little girl the best way I can and hope that one day the missing piece will be found.

I love my little girl with all my heart.

But, I loved Susie with all my soul.

December 14, 2001

"You know, Rick," Susie said over the phone, "you're not supposed to see me before the wedding."

Her words hit me like a slap in the face; stinging and making me want to cry. I had made the early morning phone call from work, excited that she would be riding in with Lisa. This would be her first time to come to work in the morning since her heart attack. She was due for a complete makeover at the salon next door to our cleaners and her appointment was for 10:00. Why not just come in and work a couple of hours beforehand, I reasoned? I called to make sure she had gotten up on time and that she was getting ready.

I heard her say it, and it saddened me. I slumped to the floor, my back against the wall and I began to question her. "What wedding, sweetie?"

"Well, our wedding, of course!"

"Susie, we're not getting married. We've been married for 21 years."

"But..." she was confused, "...well then, we're renewing our vows."

"No we're not, Susie, you're coming in to work with Lisa."

"Rick," she insisted, "we're getting married tonight. I mailed out all of the invitations; the flowers have been ordered and we have the church reserved!"

"Susie," I said, very softly, "you had a heart attack, and your brain is a little confused. Just think about it. We've been married 21 years. You renew vows on the 25th anniversary. There is nothing going on tonight."

"Yes there is, Rick. I've got the bridesmaid's dresses right behind me."

"Look behind you. See if they're there."

There was a pause. "Lisa must have taken them. Rick, I'm telling you that we're supposed to be at the church tonight. A lot of people are going to be there. I mailed out all the invitations."

She began to get upset. I had seldom seen her so adamant about anything that had confused her before. Normally she would believe me when I told her what was real and what wasn't, but this was different. She began to cry when she finally realized there was no wedding. Even at the end of the day it upset her to talk about it.

She seems more confused lately. Could her mind be retreating back to a happier time? Is this her way of dealing with her injury? Don't live in the painful present. Use your mind as a time machine and relive the past. It would be enviable to me how real it all was to her, except that it crushed her to recognize it was all a dream.

I find myself torn between feeling so very sorry for this poor woman and feeling just as sorry for myself. I honestly don't know who has it worse. At least she has the luxury of withdrawing from reality every now and then. I am faced with the continual struggle of the day-to-day certainty of my situation: I have been robbed of the love and companionship of the only woman I have ever wanted to share either with. Those who have the comfort of viewing my circumstances from the outside looking in, don't judge me too harshly. What Susie has been through and what she continues to deal with every minute of every day is horrible. What I go through, however, is no less horrible.

Susie has been relieved, at least temporarily, of taking care of herself, the kids, our business, the house, our finances, homework, cooking, cleaning, taxiing, and virtually anything else that constitutes parenting and marriage. She has only to wake up, do what I tell her needs to be done, and then go to sleep. I have to deal with all of the above and try to balance that with the agony of losing Susie. This pain never goes away. I am weary of my stomach hurting. I have to try ignoring this pain and salvaging something constructive from every day. It continues to challenge me. It doesn't get any easier.

I have well meaning family and friends who continually remind me of how well Susie has done and how far she has come. I fully realize this. But I feel like a mountain climber who has trudged 10,000 feet of a 50,000-foot summit. If I look back I see the progress, but when I look up I see how far there remains to go. The advances, which at one time were fast and furious, are now heartbreakingly slow. I wonder sometimes if Susie has the resolve to continue, or if I have the endurance. I can feel myself growing increasingly weary of the journey. But like the rabbit being chased by the fox, man, I gotta make it.

I, too, yearn for the past and happier days. At night, when Susie is asleep beside me, I close my own eyes and relive those times. I remember when all of our children would be asleep just on the other side of our door, and we would wait for the baby to wake up. Both of our alarms were set, and we would both be at work the next day. Her van was in the garage, her keys in her purse. I would leave for work before her, she would get the kids to school and then be at work with me after dropping the baby off at daycare. We would work together, eat lunch together and then come home. One son to practice. One son to get a book report done. One daughter to worry about. One wife to love at night. One very, very happy life.

But then I open my eyes and look around, and it all comes back. The weariness returns. The eternal, unremitting ache of dread and fear enters my gut. Reality, again, will make sleep nearly impossible. The overpowering sense of loneliness covers me like a blanket.

I don't write this looking for pity. I write to try and understand. I have stopped looking for answers - they don't come. Writing helps me cope with my fears and gives me something to look forward to.

I don't want a counselor to talk to me. I don't want others who have been through this to talk to me. No one has been through what I have. No one else has lost Susie. I don't want pills to help me sleep. What I want, what I need, what I long for, what I pray for is what should have never been taken from me in the first place.

What I have to do now is try and learn to live with the loss. What I must do now is attempt to give my wife and kids as normal and as happy of a life as possible. It's up to me. And to quote a line from a famous musical, I'll try, by God, I'll try.

A voice whispers, "Rick - you think you gonna make it?"

Make it? Man, I gotta make it.

"Merry Christmas," she said.

I stopped chewing, and put my fork down. "What?"

Susie looked confused for a moment, unsure of herself, then answered, "I said Merry Christmas."

"That's what I thought you said. Who were you talking to?"

She grinned at me with that beautiful smile of hers, and then laughed as she said, "I guess I was talking to my food."

And then we both laughed. I told her she was probably the first human being to wish their food, "Merry Christmas."

Thank God she can laugh at moments like these. I'm not an expert on brain injuries, but I would imagine that this could have gone either way. Susie could just as easily been afflicted with a personality that, instead of laughing at herself, would react with frustration or even violence. I'm grateful that we were blessed with passiveness.

Another example: We were backing out of our driveway the other night, and I stopped at the end of the drive so we could admire the Christmas lights that our son, Ricky, had put up. He did a great job and we acknowledged it. A couple of minutes into our journey, Susie asked me, "Rick, when are you going to take those lights down?" I looked at her, and said, "How about sometime after Christmas?"

She laughed out loud, and said, "Well, I guess that makes perfect sense, doesn't it?"

Susie can laugh at herself. Most of the time, anyway. There are times when she gets so frustrated she cries like a child, but not as often as she used to. She'll get up to do something, or I catch her standing at a doorway, and I'll ask her what she's doing, or what does she need? And she can't answer me. Her face becomes a mask of confusion, her brain trying so very hard to respond and respond intelligently, but it won't happen. All she can manage is, "I don't know, Rick. I know I got up to do something, or get something, but now I don't know what it was. Dammit, Rick! Why can't I remember?" Then, inexorably, the tears flow, and I go to her and hold her, and try to comfort her. Like a child, she puts her face into my chest, and takes comfort knowing I'm there.

I have become comfortable in this role. She has come to depend on me completely and absolutely. She doesn't like it if I'm away from her for any length of time. I find there is satisfaction when she says to me over the phone, "I want you to come home." Of course, I immediately go to her. There is no choice.

It is amazing how utterly different Susie has become. Really, there isn't the slightest remnant of what used to be. This once vibrant and independent woman has become introverted and nearly helpless. The longing and ache I feel for the past is interminable, yet there is some comfort in being this valuable to another human being. The one piece of our marriage that remains to this day is the irrefutable truth that I am the only one in the world she wants. Sadly, I am drawn to her the way a father bonds with a child. I don't want a different child, but I hunger for a mature, adult relationship. I will never be unfaithful, so there will forever be an abyss in my life that only a healed Susie can fill.

It's not all bad. We play, we tease, and we laugh. I attempt to show our kids that our marriage is sound, and that their mother is home and still their mother. I try and motivate Susie, and encourage her to participate in every day motherly duties. At times I am successful, other times not. Occasionally I observe her attempting busy work and I am optimistic. She'll clean out a pantry, straighten a linen shelf or empty the dishwasher. More often, however, she'll lie down and nap, or sleep in and let Lisa get Scotty dressed, fed and off to school.

We're trying new medicine. If this doesn't work, I'll try something else. The one thing I owe Susie is never settling for anything less than trying everything possible to help her get better. That's part of my job now - helping her get better.

I would have not chosen this new way of life. I was perfectly content with the life we had. But sometimes we are not given a choice. Did God pick me for Susie, knowing what would happen to her and also knowing I would not leave her side when she would need me most? I don't know. I don't know a lot of things these days. What I do know is that for as long as we both draw breath, we will remain together.

Lisa asked Susie what she wanted for Christmas. Susie answered that she wanted her head to get better. Is this the voice of a woman who I knew a long time ago? Is the adult Susie still in there somewhere, longing desperately to free herself from the bonds of her illness? Is there a voice whispering help me! so softly that I'm not hearing it? And will she give up, becoming too weary to continue and finding it easier, as in reality, to lie down and sleep, and let someone else, the child, become Susie?

I hope not. Because our children will eventually grow up and move away, and that will leave us with only each other.

What Susie wants for Christmas is what I want as well. I want her head to get better. I want her to say "Merry Christmas" to people. I want her to be able to get up and remember why.

Is this asking for too much? I don't think so. Our list is short and reasonable. The cost? It doesn't matter. There are things in this world that you cannot put a price on.

Things like a healthy wife, a future without fear, and a past without pain. These things, which so many are fortunate enough to have, I'll likely never have again.

Or will I?

December 24, 2001

Merry Christmas, Susie.

Have I told you what I want this year? No? Well, I've been busy these past few weeks, so I guess I forgot to tell you. So, here goes:

I would like for you to continue to get better. I look back over my writings from when you first came home and the difference is dramatic. You could remember nothing short-term, but now you remember a great deal. You are now able to recall all of our birthdays and ages. I can no longer fool you about our "new baby". You are aware of the month and year. You know that Christmas is near. So, first on my list, is for you to keep on improving.

Next, I want you to know, absolutely, that I will never leave you. Or grow tired of caring for you. Or ever, ever blame you for the way you are. You seem to worry a great deal over this. Perhaps it is because you feel so very helpless, and frustrated, and you wonder what you would do if I went away. You cry a lot about this lately, and you hold me so tightly while you beg me never to get tired of you that it utterly breaks my heart. Honey, I remain totally committed to you, and I vow to remain by your side for the rest of our lives. As God is my witness I will always be there for you.

I would also like, once again, to know peace of mind. I feel it returning, slowly but surely. I know that God is trying to explain to me why things have turned out as they have. I feel certain that one day I will understand. Until then I take comfort being able to make you safe and secure. You look at me with love, and that is satisfying. You depend on me completely, the way a very young child does, the way our children once did, and I take pleasure in this responsibility, just as I always have. You call and tell me you miss me. You tell me "I love you". I hold you while you sleep. I watch you breathe. All of these things bring me contentment and help me towards this peace of mind I seek. God will bring me the rest of the way.

I would like the strength to one day be able to remember the way you were without crying. I find myself sometimes wanting to forget the past. It would be so much easier. When I look at pictures - when I reminisce - it hurts. The pain in my gut deepens and I force myself to erase the memories. I focus only on the present and the future. I agonize over being unable to recall the past without pain. This is not the way it is supposed to work.

I would like a good night's sleep. I think, perhaps, after the holidays this will be possible. The New Year, with all its promise and hope, will arrive, and I can forget about the last one. Time will tell. Only time will tell.

Most of all, though, I want you to be happy. It's what I've wanted since the day I met you. You cry a lot, especially at the end of the day, and it saddens me. Thoughts haunt you; your tired mind imagines scenarios that could never be. You panic, envisioning yourself alone in a world that scares you; a world that, a long time ago, you faced with confidence and joy. You cling to me with unmistakable fright, until I am able to calm and soothe, and you, at long last, relax and find comfort in my arms. Arms that, as always, encircle you, protect you and reassure you that I am with you. At least for one more night. My chest is your pillow, your breathing becomes tranquil, and you are able to sleep. I remain awake, happy that I am able to soothe you, sad that I have to. My eyes remain open for a long time, my hand caresses your face, an occasional tear caresses mine.

This is my Christmas list, sweetie. Do I ask for too much? I have learned to stop asking for what I desperately want - I accept, finally, the reality of our situation. We will wait and see what next Christmas brings. Perhaps, over time, you will again face life with confidence and joy. Maybe, one day, I will again hold you at night and experience the physical closeness that only a husband and wife can. And one day, perchance, we will both be able to remember the past without pain.

I would never, ever ask for anything else again.

So, Merry Christmas, Susie. I give you my love and my life. We will wait and see what God has planned for us. On Christmas day we will celebrate life. On New Year's day we will celebrate hope. And every day, I will celebrate you.

Come what may.

December 30, 2001

I have been staring at the computer screen for almost an hour now. Both the screen, and my mind, a blank. I feel the urge to write - it is overwhelming - and yet, what do I say? What can I write that hasn't already been written?

The holidays, as I knew they would, have been nearly inconsolably dismal for me. The kids, thankfully, have enjoyed them. I hope I've been able to fool them and at least have appeared happy. I find that my mood swings are wildly erratic. I manage to cope fairly well when I am at work or otherwise away from Susie. It is when I have spent some time with her that I feel the almost excruciating despair and solitude. I have learned tolerance when I am with her, and I believe that she in no way comprehends the devastation I feel. I know that, at times, I take out my frustration on my kids. I hope they understand. I vow to not only attempt to do better, but also to make up for my impatience and undeserved resentment towards them. Shouldn't they also feel the same emotions I am? Of course not, but it remains daunting to understand this. How can they seem so happy while I fight to remain upright while balancing the roles of father, caretaker and business owner? In a selfish way, it's terribly unfair. In a righteous way, I'm glad for them.

My wife inches her way toward recovery. Susie remembers a lot of things; she forgets a lot as well. If she sees that Sean still has his basketball uniform on, even after we both had just watched him play, she will ask over and over what time he has to be at his game. She remains inward and quiet, so very different from before. It is extremely challenging to find any drive or ambition in her. I asked her only yesterday what her goals were. She said, "to grow old and happy." What about getting better? She said, "Yeah, that, too."

I wonder how much time will have to pass before I will be

able to feel some sense of happiness again? There are times now, once in a great while, that I feel hope and a sense of long lost contentment. Susie will briefly emerge from her cocoon, the beautiful butterfly I remember from long ago shyly making an appearance, only to be quickly gone again. For the most part, her speech is confused and slurred, her expressions and gestures reminiscent of those with brain injuries similar to hers. It is a harsh and cruel reminder, seemingly aimed at me every waking hour I am with her, as constant as time itself. The pangs of anguish never go away. I don't believe I will ever get used to this. Only her recovery - only the return of Susie - will bring back the joy of life that I once felt.

Garth Brooks' song, "The Dance", has a whole new meaning for me these days. I can't listen to it now without thinking of my circumstances. The essence of the lyrics are, would he have given up the special dance he and his lover shared a long time ago if he had known how things would have turned out? Would I, I wonder? If I could go back in time, would I choose to avoid the horror of now and give up my twenty years of bliss? It's a fair question. Because as wonderful as life had been up until that horrifying moment on September Fifth, what I go through now, and will continue to experience for at least the distant future, offsets that happiness. I would never give up my kids. I would never relinquish my memories. But, God, how I miss my wife.

There is a new year coming up. I'm glad. I don't like this one. Most people will remember it as the year of terrorism, New York and war. I won't. Those events linger a distant second. What I will agree with are expressions such as life as we know it forever changed, the unthinkable happened and the future is so uncertain.

Where, oh where, is my optimism? I have it still, somewhere. I can't help the depression. The grief can be so overpowering at times that it consumes me, and I have to be care-

ful when this happens to count blessings and force myself to stay hopeful. Writing helps - indeed it has almost certainly kept me sane and focused on what is important. Susie is important; my kids are as well. My life is critical to both, so it is of the essence that I am there for them. I will find the strength to keep going, and I will wake every morning determined to face another day of uncertainty. There is a reason for this. Life is predestined, isn't it? I am confident that one day I will understand.

Susie sleeps as I write this, little Scotty beside her. The house is quiet, and I am alone with my thoughts. It is so similar to years gone by. And, until Susie wakes up, I can pretend that it is as it was. The only reminder is the ever present ache of fear and dread. The fear of the unknown and the dread of the present. I still cry from time to time, sometimes at night, and sometimes in the morning as I prepare for the day. Before she wakes up.

Because, really, Susie won't wake up. Not today, and probably not for a long, long time. Her eyes will open, her body will rise, but Susie will sleep. Will she ever awaken from this slumber, so deep and so seemingly unapproachable? Only time will tell. If she does, though, I will be there to welcome her back.

Happy New Year. To the old one, good riddance. This time next year, I wonder what I will write? Maybe I will write that I kissed Susie on the lips, and her eyes opened and she said, "Good morning, Rick." And, again, I will cry.

And the ache will, at last, go away. The demons will leave. I will no longer be lonely. The zest for life will return. My kids will no longer fear undeserved resentment.

Once again, we'll dance.

EPILOGUE

It's not quite 8:15 on a Tuesday morning. I have drunk two cups of coffee, read the newspaper cover to cover and have showered and shaved. The dishwasher has completed its cycle and there is a load of laundry in the washer. The kids are either at work or school, breakfast eaten and lunch money tucked safely in backpacks. All appropriate papers have been signed and homework completed, ready to be turned in. I had to take Scotty to school. I was talking long distance to my mother and completely lost track of time. No big deal. I suddenly find myself with plenty of time. Missed school buses are no longer the crisis they once were.

Sadly, Susie and I had to sell our business; it was one of the most difficult decisions I have ever had to make. I had to face the reality that I simply could not take care of Susie, the kids, our house and our business. Something had to go. I made the right decision. The first night of my "retirement" I slept straight through - by far the most solid, restful sleep in months.

Seventy and eighty hour workweeks have been suddenly transformed into the luxury of being a stay at home parent, literally overnight. I now understand the term "work at home Mom." I am a "work at home Mr. Mom." I find myself saying, "If you don't put you clothes in the hamper, they won't get washed!" And, "If your socks are put in the dirty clothes inside out, you'll get them back inside out!" Scary stuff. I remember Susie saying these things. I thought it was silly, but now I realize the seriousness of these warnings. That's the reason I follow up with, "And I mean it, too!"

Now that my wife is unable to do the things she used to, it's my job to take over. I don't mind, really. I have learned to immediately clean up the kitchen as soon as supper is eaten. It's much easier. I have learned to do laundry every day, no matter how little there is. I load the dishwasher even if there is only a cup and two forks in the sink. I sweep the kitchen floor while waiting for water to boil. I make tea before we run out. I make the boys clean their rooms every day. I check Scotty's backpack for homework or instructions as soon as he walks in the door.

Susie has trouble getting up in the mornings. It's a shame. I love getting the boys off to school, especially Sean and Scotty. They both seem to appreciate our change in lifestyle. They love having me home in the mornings. They seem always glad to see me when they get home in the afternoons. They understand how difficult it was to sell our business, and they both gladly pitch in with chores and work that I do at home. They are really good kids. I'm glad that they will now have years of memories of me being home most of the time.

There are times, of course, when I miss the challenge of owning and operating a successful small business. But, I nearly lost my wife, and the kids their mom. Susie's heart attack changed our lives instantly and everlastingly. She may never be the same. Our future certainly won't. The sale of our business pales in comparison.

There are silver linings. I have the immense satisfaction of having written this book. It seems to have already touched and changed lives. There's not a feeling quite like it. Susie would be glad to know this not so small consolation. I am also able to attend school meetings, participate in band boosters, meet Scotty for lunch and then read to his class after. I have completed long overdue projects at home. Sean is able to play in a semi-competitive baseball league. He'll have lots of practices, games and tournaments. So what? I can take him. I have time now.

And, suddenly, I learned that time is extraordinarily valuable. Most of us take it for granted. I know that I did. What most of us see as seemingly limitless days, weeks, months and even years ahead of us, I see as a gift. What is here today may very well be gone tomorrow. Plan for the future but don't assume that it's a guarantee.

I now feel that God is taking care of my family, and is showing me that I will one day understand why all of this happened. Or at least that it is not all bad. I was working in my garage a few weeks ago, and Susie, Sean and Scotty were all in there with me. It was an unseasonably warm winter afternoon and Sean had found a baseball, his glove and bat. Then, somehow, Scotty had managed to find his glove as well. They were throwing the ball to Susie, and she would alternate throwing the ball back to the boys. Sean asked me if I would hit fly balls to them in the cove, you know, the way I used to. I told him no.

"Why not?" he logically responded. And for some reason, I couldn't think of one single excuse why not. I was just so accustomed to saying no, because I was too tired or didn't have time, or some other justification, that it just came out as "no." So I stopped what I was doing, grabbed the bat, and for the next 45 minutes I hit fly balls to two gleefully happy young sons of mine. The grins nearly broke their faces in two. And I'm telling you, if anyone would have asked them who was the greatest Dad - or Mr. Mom - in the world, the vote would have been two to nothing, at least in that moment of extremely precious time.

The culmination of all of this came when little Scotty finally caught a high fly ball for the first time. After cheers from his brother and me, he yelled with absolute sincerity, "Man, Dad, this is the greatest day of my life!"

The greatest day of his life. And I was not only there to share it with him, but I had everything to do with it. And there is not a doubt in this world that, had circumstances not changed our lives, we would all have been at work, the two of them watching television and waiting for the hours to pass to, finally, go home.

I have difficulty adjusting to my new life at times. I still experience the inexorable melancholy occasionally. But I am my kid's Dad again. I may not be an important business owner, but I have reclaimed the role of being important in a far more significant undertaking.

I am Dad. Hear me roar.

Still, it is with a little sadness that I come to the end of this book. I wrote this book, and these journals, because I enjoyed it immensely and it was extremely therapeutic. These past few months they have been a large reason I've been able to maintain my sanity. Writing thoughts and emotions down, rather than keeping them bottled up inside, is comforting and necessary.

I am very fortunate. That sounds a little strange coming from me. I have lived the last few months in a world that has been turned upside down. Yet, I look back and reflect on the events that changed everything and, somehow, I feel blessed. I am, at last, at peace. I harbor no ill feelings towards God or man. I feel gratitude towards all who contributed to Susie's recovery. I am closer to my family than I have ever been. I am enormously relieved that I am able to feel this way. It could so easily have gone bad.

For a period of time, I drank too much. There was a time in my life where I wondered if I would ever feel happy or contented again. I existed in a bubble whose walls were so fragile the slightest irritation would cause it to burst. I would become enraged and out of control. I nearly lost loved ones who are very dear to me. Thank God I saw what was happening to me in time.

There were also events which occurred that very nearly broke my will and my faith. I chose not to include it in this book, although initially I wrote two chapters recounting what happened. Eventually I decided that it had the potential to cause Susie and my children further grief, and I concluded that they had suffered enough. Also, those involved have worked hard to rebuild damaged relationships, as I have, and I wish to maintain these relationships. They are important to me, and I can't let anger or revenge override what makes obvious sense. At the time, the pain was crushing and seemingly everlasting, and the nightmares from it return on rare occasions, but I have learned that unimaginable pain can cause people to do and say things that otherwise would have been unthinkable. I have to believe that at no other time would their actions have been possible.

Time. The great healer. The passage of time has contributed extensively to closing wounds that I thought were permanent. Mercifully, I am, for the most part, unable to remember the way Susie was before her heart attack. Equally merciful is she has improved greatly in the months since she's been home. She now helps with the cooking and the cleaning on occasion. She folds the laundry and puts away the clothes. She is wonderful at putting on makeup and getting dressed. She is eager to go with me to take the boys to baseball practice and to their games, and loves watching them. She no longer hedges on taking walks with me. She loves to hold my hand. She kisses me often.

Still, I remain dreadfully lonely for Susie from time to time - the Susie I fell in love with and married so many years ago. That Susie no longer exists. I have a new Susie now. Like a child, I love her in a non-physical way. It's such a shame. She remains unable to drive or care for herself. She is lethargic and sleeps a lot. I find myself alone a lot of the time. She seems to have hit a wall in her recovery. While she is vastly improved from when she first came home, I have seen little progress in the past three or four months. I have resigned myself to accepting that what we have is all we may get. Good enough. It is certainly better than burying her. Occasionally, though, the grief can still be overwhelming.

But I will rebound somehow. We have far too many years of our lives left to remain brooding over something we can't change. I will continue writing journal entries. They help me cope, and it is interesting to look back over these writings from a long time ago. It is a very good way to see just how far Susie has come since her homecoming from the hospital, reminders that are good for the soul in times of despondency that are inevitable now and then.

I have my family, my faith and my resolve to keep me going. I don't cry anymore about the unfairness of it all. Who said life is fair anyway? Like Susie, I have good and bad days. I'm almost used to the way Susie is now. The memories of how she was are fading. I look at pictures and the pain returns. I refuse to look at videos. I don't ever picture myself able to watch them again.

Will I ever enjoy life the way I used to? This early on, I have no idea. Thank God I have my kids to keep me going. They are the reason for my being. I take enormous pride in them - most of the time anyway. I don't know what I would do without them.

I pray for Susie, and for my family, every night. I ask God to watch over her, and to continue giving me strength. The fear of the unknown is still very real. But the Bible reminds us to "fear no evil, for Thou art with me." That's good enough for me.

I love my wife. That's the bottom line. I love my family. The most important thing in the world right now is that my wife, and my family, are all here with me inside our home. Money, the business we had to sell - countless aspects of our old life - are so insignificant now that I have trouble even remembering them. I have plans for the future that would have been out of the question prior to September Fifth. I relish the challenges the future holds. Bring it on. I can't help but believe these challenges pale in comparison to the last several months.

The roller coaster ride is, at long last, over. I firmly believe that the operator, when he finally stopped the cars to let me out, nodded and saluted in respect. I had survived, despite his best efforts to toss me off the ride prematurely. The demons have, for the most part, given up and left. The ache in my stomach has disappeared except on rare occasions. I sleep soundly most nights.

I have to live. There are too many people counting on me and I will not let them down. I am satisfied with what I have. If God sees fit to bless Susie further, what a bonus! If not, I will scoop her up in my arms as she is, and I will carry her lovingly through the rest of our years with pride and compassion.

Could things be better? I guess. Could things be worse? Of course. There is not a person alive who could answer these questions differently. So, it's either dwell on what could have been or reach for what will be. I prefer to reach.

Words on paper. They have sustained me for a long time. I have embraced and depended on them. I am grateful to God for having the ability to write what I feel. And what I feel, most of all, is relief.

We are fam - i - ly.

You all know the rest of it.

Rick and Susie live in Bartlett, Tennessee where they have lived for the past 17 years. Rick is a past columnist for their local newspaper, and has done motivational and customer service seminars in the United States and Canada. Rick welcomes feedback, and his home and e-mail address are located on the information page at the beginning of this book.